ALEXANDRA STYRON

STEAL *this* COUNTRY

a HANDBOOK for RESISTANCE, PERSISTENCE, and FIXING ^almost EVERYTHING

VIKING

VIKING
An imprint of Penguin Random House LLC
375 Hudson Street
New York, New York 10014

First published in the United States of America by Viking,
an imprint of Penguin Random House LLC, 2018

LIBRARY OF CONGRESS CATALOGING-IN-PUBLICATION DATA
Names: Styron, Alexandra, author.
Title: Steal this country : a handbook for resistance, persistence, and fixing almost everything /
by Alexandra Styron.
Description: New York : Viking, [2018] |
Identifiers: LCCN 2017060705 (print) | LCCN 2018001593 (ebook) | ISBN 9780451479396 (ebook) |
ISBN 9780451479372 (hardcover)
Subjects: LCSH: Youth—Political activity—United States. | Community organization—United States. |
Social action—United States.
Classification: LCC HQ799.2.P6 (ebook) | LCC HQ799.2.P6 S79 2018 (print) |
DDC 320.0835/0973—dc23
LC record available at https://lccn.loc.gov/2017060705

Printed in China   Book design by Kate Renner

10 9 8 7 6 5 4 3 2 1

For Huck and Martha,
my North Stars

Change will not come if we wait for some other person
or if we wait for some other time. We are the ones we've
been waiting for. We are the change that we seek.

–Barack Obama

CONTENTS

THE WHY

· · · · · · · · · · · · · · · ·

A Note from Me to You

Dear Readers,

Before we get down to business, I want to tell you a little about how and why this book came to be.

Very late on the night of November 8, 2016, I crawled into bed feeling like I might barf. My daughter Martha had finally fallen asleep. My husband Ed and our son Huck were still downstairs, flipping between CNN, MSNBC, and ABC. They were hoping, I guess, for a different outcome from the one that was fast becoming inevitable: Donald J. Trump was going to be the forty-fifth president of the United States.

Me, I couldn't watch. I've always had a tendency to look away when things are upsetting or scary. I can't really watch horror movies. Or if I do, it's usually through the weave of the blanket I've put over my head. And as far as I was concerned, the election was a horror movie. Kind of like the end of *Carrie*, the film based on the Stephen King novel. (If you haven't watched it, I won't spoil it, but trust me . . . *you just don't see it coming*.)

Like practically everyone else, I had been certain that Hillary Clinton was going to win that night. All the polls showed her with a comfortable lead. She had crushed every debate. And, as a former senator and secretary of state, she was way more qualified than Donald Trump, a reality TV show host who literally lived in a golden tower and knew nothing about policy or how most Americans lived. Then there was the issue of character. Hillary had devoted her entire career to working for child welfare, universal healthcare, and world diplomacy. Donald had spent his career discriminating against minorities, demeaning women, and mocking the disabled. I mean, no contest, right?

Wrong.

Cue the soundtrack from *Psycho*. It was going to be a long night.

I grew up in a family of social activists. My father, who was a well-known novelist, frequently used his public stature to address issues of racial inequality, campaign for free speech, and come to the defense of prisoners who were sentenced unjustly. When I was five years old, my mother got involved with Amnesty International, an organization that was still new in the United States. She soon became a passionate human rights activist. At our town hall in 1972, I slipped under the curtain of the voting booth and hugged my mom's knee when she cast her ballot for George McGovern (he lost to Richard Nixon). I wasn't exactly a red diaper baby (that's what they used to call the children of Communists), but I was definitely raised left of center.

But I was also raised in the 1980s. Marketers call us—me and your parents, probably—Generation X. But they might as well call us Generation W. As in Wack. For most of my teenage years, Ronald Reagan was president, greed was good (see *Wall Street*, the movie, 1987), and yuppies strode the planet in shoulder pads that could intimidate a linebacker. Squeezed between hippie baby boomers and skeptical millennials, Gen Xers are known for being a conservative, apathetic, and negative-minded generation. When I was in high school, politics was a footnote in the school paper and no one protested anything—except that time the cafeteria replaced the mayonnaise with Miracle Whip.

Then I went to college at Columbia University and a cool thing happened. It was 1985, and seven fellow students, angered by our school's financial investments in South Africa during the apartheid era, decided to fast in protest. When the university refused to hear their demands, the students chained an administrative building shut and refused to move. Their protest quickly grew, eventually turning into an encampment of thousands of students demanding divestment, boycotting classes, and sleeping on cardboard in the center of campus.

I joined the protest early on, and clocked a lot of hours chanting and debating and trying to find a comfortable position on the brick walkway. Protesting wasn't a hardship. Apartheid was a hardship. Protesting was thrilling, because it was important. As the writer Alice Walker says, "Resistance is the secret of joy." There was joy in what we were doing. Making noise, sticking our thumbs in the eye of the administration, speaking truth to power. And the joy caused people to listen. All the major news outlets carried the story of our action. Similar protests began springing up at other universities. Four months after the end of the blockade, Columbia's board of trustees voted to divest more than $32 million worth of holdings in companies doing business in South Africa. The cascading effect of this and other corporate divestment had a huge impact on the South African economy. Divestment helped bring an end to that country's racist political system in the early 1990s.

On the night of the last election, I tossed and slept an hour, maybe two, and woke up thinking of those college days. Then I went downstairs to get my kids off to school. When Martha came down, she began to cry, just as she had done when she went to sleep. At eleven years old, she was, and is, a deeply moral person, and a hard-core feminist. Hillary's campaign office was next door to her school; Martha and her friends had done a lot of phone banking and participated in a campaign video. She was devastated. Huck, two years older than his sister, appeared a few minutes later, weary and angry. He was originally a Bernie

Sanders volunteer, but had gotten right on board for Hillary after she won the nomination. The week before the election, our family drove to Pennsylvania to encourage people to vote. Some folks shut the door in our faces, or pointed at the Trump stickers on their bumpers. But most people were glad to see us. We drove back home tired but stoked, oblivious to the bubble around us. Now that bubble had popped, and it felt like we'd been in a car crash.

Let me tell you a secret: sometimes parents have no idea what to say. Inside, we still feel like teenagers ourselves. Some days we look in the mirror and think, "Whoa, who's that grown-up looking back at me?" And it's kind of scary when we need to come up with answers for our kids and we don't have any good ones at the ready. I didn't have any good ones that morning. So this is what I said: This sucks. In a big way. But whatever happens, this election will probably define much of who you become. It may even affect what you decide to do with your life. Things are going to be different after this. So you're going to have to figure out how to make different *better*.

That sounded OK, for Huck and Martha. But what was *I* going to do? Well, I decided to write this book. I guess it's my form of activism. A successful movement is kind of like a potluck dinner party. Everyone should bring their best dish. Writing is what I know how to do, so that's what I've brought to the party. I also brought my awesome niece Lilah Larson, who is a kick-ass research assistant and musician. She contributed a lot to the pages in here. If you think they're cool, it's because of her. If they're dorky, it's on me.

But *Steal This Country* is also another kind of offering. To Huck and Martha—and to you. It's a way of making amends. Because Generation W totally let you down. Too many of us weren't paying attention. Weren't passionate enough. Weren't focused enough. We fell asleep at the wheel, and we let the car crash. Many of us feel very bad about that, and are doing our best to fix the mess. But we definitely can't do it without you.

I know you guys won't make the same mistake. Because you're members of an amazing generation. Tolerant, generous, innovative, and, after this last election, I hope ready to rumble.

You *are* reading this book, after all.

I hope you enjoy it, learn from it, and most of all, use it to make different *better*.

introduction

On Making Good Trouble, Finding Joy, and Getting Down with the Underground Fungus

One day in 1970, a guy named Abbie Hoffman started writing a book. Hoffman was a true rebel. Smart, righteous, and big on theatrics, he made a name for himself as a kind of professional disrupter during the protest movements of the 1960s. In fact, at the moment he started writing, he was sitting in a jail cell, on trial for his role in the violence that shook Chicago during the 1968 Democratic Convention.

You've probably heard about the summer of '68. It was a pretty messed-up time. The United States was in the middle of a long, bloody, and unpopular war in Vietnam. The struggle for civil rights raged on. Dr. Martin Luther King Jr. had been assassinated. So had Senator Robert F. Kennedy. All over the country, college students and other protestors were marching against war and injustice, risking their safety, demanding to be heard. Hoffman, a cofounder of the Youth International Party, aka the Yippies, had urged his followers to come to Chicago for their own alternate "convention." That August, thousands of passionate activists descended on the city, where they were confronted by a massive show of force from police and

National Guardsmen. Peaceful protest turned quickly to heated violence. Hundreds of people on both sides were injured; hundreds were also arrested. Abbie Hoffman and six other organizers were charged with multiple offenses, including crossing state lines to incite a riot.

While the "Chicago Seven" awaited their verdict, Hoffman wrote the first pages of *Steal This Book*. It was a manifesto of sorts, aimed at young people, in which he suggested various ways to fight the Establishment. That included the government, big business, parents, basically everyone with power. Some of his advice was practical: what to wear to demonstrations, how to organize in your city. Some of it was provocative: how to Dumpster dive for free food, how to start an underground press. And some—how to shoplift, ways to make a homemade bomb—was totally bananas, and also illegal.

Hoffman had a very hard time getting his book published. And when he did, many bookstores didn't want to carry it because people kept *stealing the book*. Somehow, though, Hoffman's work became a best seller, which was ironic: mainstream success didn't exactly fit his counterculture image.

There's been a lot of talk recently about the 1960s. Because once again, it's getting real. The 2016 election was, we now know, compromised by interference by Russia. President Donald Trump won the electoral college by seventy-seven votes, but lost the popular vote by a margin of almost three million. Since taking control of the White House, the new administration has pushed legislation that discriminates against Muslims, threatens women's health, diminishes LGBTQIA rights, marginalizes immigrants, defunds arts institutions, rolls back education standards, harms the environment, and takes meals from hungry children. President Trump has advocated for the repeal of a healthcare system that insures millions of hardworking citizens, and he's moving us dangerously close to a nuclear standoff with North Korea.

Just as in the '60s, it feels like the people in control of things are operating outside our best interests. They don't understand us and they don't care about the things that matter to us.

Has all of this stuff made you angry? Good. It ought to.

But don't let that anger make you feel helpless—because you're not.

Yes, old people got the country into this mess. But you can help get us out. And though you may not be able to vote yet, your voice can still be heard. It should be heard!

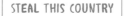

Let's be clear: we're not recommending you blow stuff up. In fact, we like this quote from Dr. Martin Luther King Jr.: "Nonviolence is a powerful and just weapon that cuts without wounding and ennobles the man who wields it. It is a sword that heals."

Still, we think Hoffman was onto something. Like all great rebels, radicals, and revolutionaries, he understood that morality is mightier than authority, and that there are times when you have to do a few things "wrong" in order to make a lot of things right. The great civil rights hero and Georgia congressman John Lewis calls it getting into "good trouble." "Sometimes," he says, "you have to get in the way."

In the pages ahead, you'll hear about all kinds of people who have gotten themselves into good trouble. People who stood up, sat down, walked out. Who spoke up when silence was expected; who told the truth when it would have been much easier to lie. Some troublemakers have gone to prison. Some have risked their lives. Many of them are leaders who became famous for their efforts. Many more are foot soldiers in the struggle whose contributions are no less important. And they all share a few familiar characteristics:

They were teenagers once. Just like you.

They were curious. Just like you.

They were thoughtful. Just like you.

The people you'll read about in *Steal This Country* also share another thing: they've all seen injustice in the world around them and instead of being paralyzed by despair, they became energized by hope. Positive change requires hope. It's the spark that lights the flame. To make a difference, you have to believe that better things are possible, even if attaining them means long or hard work.

Which brings us to fungus. The writer and activist Rebecca Solnit uses an interesting metaphor to talk about the way social justice movements work. "After a rain," she says, "mushrooms appear on the surface of the earth as if from nowhere. Many do so from a sometimes vast underground fungus that remains invisible and largely unknown." Great movements are similar. Everything seems quiet and orderly and then— boom!—four-million-plus people are demonstrating in Women's Marches all over the globe. As Solnit points out, it appears "spontaneous" but in truth "less visible long-term organizing and groundwork—or underground work—often laid the foundation."

A lot of this book is devoted to the fungus. We've explored dozens of ways to engage in social activism. Some of them are splashy and fast and will get lots of attention; other methods require organizing and planning and long-term commitments. We like to think you'll be interested in both. Because mushrooms are awesome on the surface, but they can't thrive without the fungus underneath.

That doesn't mean activism is dark and dreary! On the contrary, all that good trouble and hard work and hope should also add up to joy. Joy in being part of a movement, joy in the sense of belonging to a community, joy in living your life with purpose, joy in the knowledge that the world will be better for your passion and your commitment.

Joy is not the same thing as fun. It's deeper than fun. More exciting, too. And if that spark of hope catches, what's to stop you from setting the world on fire?

THE WHO

Social activism in the United States has a long and proud history. In fact, you could argue the country was founded by activists, since the Revolutionary War was basically a giant act of protest. And we Americans have been agitating for change ever since. The freedom to protest against injustice, to defend what we believe in, and to speak up for ourselves and for others is not only essential to our national character, it's essential to our democracy.

There are thousands of great American protest stories. Check out these amazing moments of heroic activism in our young history, as well as some heroic young activists who have made history . . . amazing!

a few
GREAT
MOMENTS
in *US PROTEST*
HISTORY

BOSTON TEA PARTY, 1773

Fed up with being taxed for goods but having no representation in Parliament, an angry group of colonists dressed up like Native Americans and looted merchant ships, tossing cases of tea into Boston Harbor. The protest caused the British to shut down Boston Harbor and take away the Massachusetts colony's right to self-govern. The colonists' response: organize an army and take a stand for independence! Emerging from the Revolutionary War victorious, the Founding Fathers drew up the United States Constitution and its Bill of Rights, which ensures, among other rights, the freedom of assembly and the freedom of speech.

PROTEST. IT'S THE AMERICAN WAY!

THE DESTRUCTION OF TEA AT BOSTON HARBOR.

FREDERICK DOUGLASS PUBLISHES HIS FIRST AUTOBIOGRAPHY, 1845

Seven years after escaping slavery, twenty-seven-year-old Frederick Douglass published *Narrative of the Life of Frederick Douglass, an American Slave, Written by Himself.* The book solidified his status as a great thinker and activist and was a best seller at the time, with five thousand copies sold within a few months.

Douglass was a gifted public speaker and a magnetic presence; his speeches in the United States and Europe arguing for the abolition of slavery drew large crowds.

Using money from his speaking tours, Douglass published a newspaper, the

North Star, which advocated for both African American and women's rights. His paper's motto was "**RIGHT IS OF NO SEX—TRUTH IS OF NO COLOR.**" Douglass's elegant writing and fiery speeches would make him a powerful political figure and one of the greatest visionaries of the nineteenth century.

SENECA FALLS CONVENTION, 1848

Over tea at a neighbor's, housewife, mother, and abolitionist Elizabeth Cady Stanton detailed her discontent with the state of women's rights in America. The other women there felt the same way. They decided to convene a meeting to discuss "the social, civil, and religious condition and rights of woman." They also drew up a Declaration of Sentiments, using the Declaration of Independence as inspiration. Stanton added a controversial resolution: **A DEMAND FOR WOMEN'S SUFFRAGE**, or the right to vote.

The announcement of the meeting in local papers drew an estimated three hundred women and men to the first Women's Rights Convention, held at Wesleyan Chapel in Seneca Falls, New York. Stanton argued eloquently for her suffrage clause; Frederick Douglass, also in attendance, had her back on this. Still, the idea of women voting was so forward thinking, even some of the women at the convention were scandalized

and rejected the demand as too outrageous. The Declaration of Sentiments passed, though the suffrage resolution squeaked by with only a two-vote majority. It would take seventy-two more years until women's suffrage was the law of the land. But the women's rights movement had officially begun.

MARCH OF THE MILL CHILDREN, 1903

Protesting long work hours and brutal working conditions, more than one hundred thousand textile workers in Philadelphia went on strike in the summer of 1903. Many of the strikers were children, more than sixteen thousand of whom worked in mills in and around the city. The laborers' rights crusader Mary Harris "Mother" Jones hatched a plan to march one hundred miles with several hundred children and their parents to President Theodore Roosevelt's summer home in New York and make their voices heard. The march began on July 7 in the sweltering heat. The speeches Jones delivered at stops along the way, as well as the spectacle of the marching children, **AWAKENED THE NATION TO THE MISERY OF CHILD LABOR.** Nearly three weeks later, the march reached New York City. To dramatize their abuse at the hands of bosses, Mother Jones staged an exhibit at Coney Island of some of the children in cages. She took a small delegation to the president's home on Long Island. Though Roosevelt refused to meet with the demonstrators, within a few years Pennsylvania changed its labor laws in favor of children. And in 1938, Roosevelt's distant cousin, President Franklin Roosevelt, signed the Fair Labor Standards Act, which provides comprehensive protections for child workers.

THE BIRMINGHAM CHILDREN'S CRUSADE, 1963

Beginning on May 2, hundreds of young people marched from the Sixteenth Street Baptist Church to downtown Birmingham, Alabama, to protest segregation in a city that had become "ground zero" in the struggle for civil rights. The march was organized by Reverend James Bevel of the Southern Christian Leadership Conference (SCLC). He coached the kids on the principles of nonviolence espoused by Dr. Martin Luther King Jr. Out in the streets, the marchers faced police, attack dogs, and fire hoses under the authority of Eugene "Bull" Connor, the city's infamous Commissioner of Public Safety. The kids sang to calm their nerves, and knelt and prayed when the police closed in. Over the course of a week, **MORE THAN A THOUSAND CHILDREN WERE ARRESTED AND JAILED.** Press coverage shocked the world, helping to turn public sentiment in the movement's favor. Birmingham's business and civic leaders ultimately acceded to many of the SCLC's demands. The Children's Crusade is widely considered a turning point in the national campaign for racial equality.

EUGENE KEYES BURNS HIS DRAFT CARD, 1963

On Christmas Eve, twenty-two-year-old Eugene Keyes participated in a twelve-hour vigil in front of the draft board office in Champaign, Illinois, where men were conscripted for military duty. Setting his draft card on fire, he used the flame to light a candle "for peace on earth." Keyes's action coincided with a growing resistance movement against the Vietnam War. At massive demonstrations in San Francisco, Minneapolis, Chicago, Boston, and other cities, young men increasingly used their draft cards as a symbol of protest. In May 1964, crowds gathered for a draft-card

burning ceremony in New York City's Union Square. In 1965, under a new amendment to the Selective Service Act (the draft), David Miller became the first man to be arrested for burning his card. And in 1966, David Harris mailed his card back to the draft board, for which **HE SPENT TWENTY MONTHS IN JAIL.** These protests and many other brave acts of defiance would eventually help bring an end to the longest US conflict in the twentieth century.

ACT UP SEIZES CONTROL OF THE FDA, 1988

In the early 1980s, human immunodeficiency virus (HIV, which causes Acquired Immunodeficiency Syndrome, or AIDS) was identified as it spread throughout the United States, taking a particularly savage toll on gay men. The Reagan administration's slow response to the epidemic inspired the formation of activist groups like the AIDS Coalition to Unleash Power (ACT UP). In one of ACT UP's earliest and most successful events, **1,500 DEMONSTRATORS BLOCKED THE FOOD AND DRUG ADMINISTRATION** (FDA) in Rockville, Maryland. The group demanded that experimental drugs to fight HIV/AIDS be made available more quickly and fairly. The protest drew large-scale media coverage and caught the public's attention during the early stages of the crisis. After the demonstration, the FDA became significantly more responsive to the needs of AIDS patients. Using creative applications of resistance to apply pressure to the National Institutes of Health, the Catholic Church, and the news media, ACT UP became a leading voice in the AIDS movement.

JULIA BUTTERFLY HILL LIVES IN A TREE, 1997–1999

In protest of the Pacific Lumber Company's plan to clear-cut some of the oldest trees in the world, Julia Hill climbed a giant California redwood in Humboldt County, California, and refused to leave. The tree, known as "Luna," was 1,500 years old and 180 feet tall. Hill spent **738 DAYS LIVING ON TWO SIX-BY-SIX-FOOT PLATFORMS** nestled in the tree's trunk. She endured freezing rains, buzzing by helicopters, and threats from angry loggers. As a condition of ending her occupa-

tion, Hill (who chose the nickname Butterfly as a child) secured an agreement by Pacific Lumber to preserve Luna and all other trees within a two-hundred-foot perimeter. She and other eco-warriors like her became heroes of the environmental movement. Their hands-on activism drew crucial attention to the adverse human impact on our planet and its resources.

COLIN KAEPERNICK AND ERIC REID TAKE A KNEE, 2016

At a preseason game, San Francisco 49ers Colin Kaepernick and Eric Reid each put one knee down on the field during the official singing of the national anthem. Prior to taking a knee, Kaepernick sat quietly during the anthem at other games as a form of protest against the oppression of people of color and against police brutality. Kaepernick told the press, **"WHEN THERE'S SIGNIFICANT CHANGE AND I FEEL THE FLAG REPRESENTS WHAT IT'S SUPPOSED TO REPRESENT . . . I'LL STAND."** Kaepernick's action inspired athletes in

many different sports to demonstrate as well. But after the 2016 season, he became a free agent and was not signed by another football team. In 2017, President Trump weighed in with insulting, derogatory remarks, and the issue of how patriotism is expressed became a major national discussion. In response to Trump's divisiveness, many professional athletes and team owners joined Kaepernick's movement and #TakeAKnee exploded on social media.

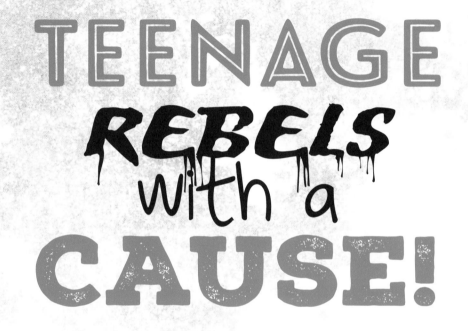

SYBIL LUDINGTON

Listen, my children, and you shall hear, of the midnight ride of . . . Sybil Ludington? That's right. Two years after Paul Revere galloped from Boston and into the history books, a sixteen-year-old badass named Sybil Ludington made a similar trek, except she went even farther and in much more challenging conditions.

On the evening of April 26, 1777, a man on horseback arrived at the Ludington farm in Dutchess County, New York. He brought news that across the Connecticut border, thousands of British troops were laying siege to the town of Danbury. Sybil's father was a colonel in General Washington's army. He needed to organize his regiment and devise a battle plan. But who could spread the call to arms to his soldiers?

Sybil. That's who.

Sybil Ludington rode nearly forty miles that night, alone and in the rain, to rouse her father's men. She raced through thick woods and villages, carrying a stick to fend off enemies who would block her progress. When she returned home, soaking wet and exhausted, more than four hundred troops had gathered and were on their way to Danbury. She had ridden twice as far as Paul Revere and in far more treacherous territory.

Why is Sybil Ludington not better known? Maybe because her father's troops arrived too late to save Danbury, so the effort isn't remembered as a victory. Or maybe because she was a kid, and a girl one at that. Never mind. We can honor her now, as part of a long tradition of teenagers crushing it in the name of freedom.

ALEXANDER HAMILTON

Born in the West Indies, Alexander Hamilton started life without much. His parents were never married and his father abandoned the family when Hamilton was still a boy. Soon, he was apprenticed to a local merchant. When he was eleven, his mother died. Orphaned and virtually penniless, Hamilton continued to work hard, despite

the fact that he sometimes hated his job. Impressed by his skills, local businessmen raised funds to send him to New York for a proper education. In 1773, Hamilton arrived at King's College (now Columbia University). He was sixteen years old.

Meantime, a revolution was brewing. In September 1774, delegates from the thirteen colonies convened the First Continental Congress in Philadelphia. The meeting produced guidelines for economic rebellion, laying the groundwork for eventual independence from British rule. Hamilton wasted no time jumping into the fray. His pamphlet *A Full Vindication of the Measures of Congress* was published during his second year at college; another followed the next year. Hamilton earned a reputation as a thinker and a firebrand.

At eighteen, he joined the Continental army and went to battle. By the time he was twenty, he was General Washington's right-hand man, writing his letters and advising on strategy. Hamilton grew tired of his desk job and the general let him return to the field. In October of 1781, Hamilton led troops into the Battle of Yorktown, a victory for American and French troops that would lead to the beginning of peace negotiations and colonial independence.

After the war, Hamilton became a member of the Continental Congress, a signer of the Constitution, and the first United States secretary of the treasury.

Nowadays, Hamilton is known as the unlikely protagonist of a smash hit on Broadway. But before he was a hip-hop hero, he was a real live teenager who believed in himself, and knew how to get things done!

CLAUDETTE COLVIN

If you know anything about the civil rights movement, then you've probably heard of Rosa Parks. Her brave refusal to give up her seat to a white passenger on a Montgomery, Alabama, bus is considered one of the most significant moments in civil rights history.

What you might not know is that nine months earlier, a fifteen-year-old girl did pretty much the exact same thing.

Claudette Colvin, a bold and inquisitive student, was on her way home from school. When she got on the bus, she took a seat in a "Colored" row. Black people were not allowed to sit in the "Whites Only" section; they were also expected to give up their seats if that section was full. Claudette sat with three other women as the bus filled up until, at last, the only seats left were in the back half of the bus. When a white woman got on board, the bus driver told Claudette's row of passengers to move to the rear. The other women complied, but Claudette refused. As she once told a reporter, "History had me glued to the seat." Claudette was taken away in handcuffs.

What happened next says a lot about the complexity of the fight for racial equality back then. With the backing of activists like Martin Luther King Jr., Claudette was prepared to challenge the city's segregation laws in court. Hundreds of letters from around the country were sent in support of her case, most of which arrived at the National Association for the Advancement of Colored People (NAACP) offices in Montgomery, where Rosa Parks was the secretary. Trained in nonviolence, Ms. Parks was also friends with white people in the city who were sympathetic to the cause. So, in the end, black leaders decided that the older woman was a safer bet to win a case that could change history. "Let Rosa be the one," Claudette's mother said to her. "White people aren't going to bother Rosa—her skin is lighter than yours and they like her."

A few months later, Rosa Parks would ride a Montgomery bus right into the history books. Claudette moved to New York, became a nurse's aide, and never talked much about her moment in history. In fact, it was not until 2009, when Phillip Hoose's book *Claudette Colvin: Twice Toward Justice* won the National Book Award for Young People's Literature, that many people knew her name at all. But that didn't diminish her impact. Like that of many unsung heroes, Claudette's courage was a crucial paving stone on the road to change.

SYLVIA RIVERA

In large part, the history of the Lesbian, Gay, Bisexual, Trangender, Queer, Intersex, Asexual (LGBTQIA) movement begins with the Stonewall riots. If that's news to you, here's a recap: the Stonewall Inn in New York's Greenwich Village was one of the centers of LGBTQIA night-life and community in the 1960s. In the early morning hours of June 28, 1969, the police, as part of an ongoing effort to shut down gay nightlife, used a liquor license issue to raid the bar. But this time the Stonewall patrons—who were tired of being harassed and fed up with police brutality—fought back. The riots lasted for five days. Seventeen-year-old Sylvia Rivera was on the front lines and was reportedly heard to say on the scene, "I'm not missing a minute of this—it's the revolution!" Her work didn't stop there.

Born Ray Rivera in the Bronx in 1951, and assigned male at birth, Sylvia was the child of a Venezuelan mother and Puerto Rican father. Her home life was turbulent, and she left when she was just eleven, moving onto the streets of Manhattan, where she was embraced by a community of drag queens. Her early years struggling to survive along with other homeless queer youth would forever shape her politics. In the immediate aftermath of the Stonewall riots, Sylvia joined the newly formed Gay Liberation Front and the Gay Activists Alliance. But these largely white, middle-class, and cisgender organizations felt alienating for someone like Sylvia—transgender and Latinx out on the streets. So, along with her friend Marsha P. Johnson, she formed Street Transvestite Action Revolutionaries (STAR). The group worked to shelter queer homeless teens like Sylvia who, because of their income, race, or gender identity, were overlooked by the more mainstream gay rights organizations.

Sylvia worked tirelessly for gay rights and for trans inclusion in the gay rights movement for the rest of her life. Her legacy lives on today in the Sylvia Rivera Law Project, which works for the right of all people to freely self-determine and express gender, regardless of race or income, and without fear.

RYAN WHITE

Ryan White was born in Kokomo, Indiana, on December 6, 1971, and diagnosed with hemophilia, a genetic disorder that keeps blood cells from clotting. Throughout his childhood, Ryan was treated with plasma transfusions. In 1984, when he was thirteen, doctors discovered that Ryan had acquired immunodeficiency syndrome, or AIDS, which he got from one of those transfusions.

In the early 1980s, AIDS was a mystery. Initially called "gay cancer," the illness moved swiftly and devastatingly through the US homosexual population. And because homophobia was a much bigger problem than it is now, the disease fueled a climate of fear and bigotry around those who suffered from it. Ryan's story was unusual. At the time, people did not understand how AIDS was spread. Many people believed that AIDS could only be transmitted through homosexual sex, or even that being gay caused the disease. Many others thought you could get AIDS by touching or just being near someone who had it.

After his diagnosis, Ryan was told he probably wouldn't live more than six months. Still, he wanted to return to school. But the school wasn't having it—people were afraid of Ryan. So his parents fought back and sued the Kokomo school district.

The White case took months to get through the Indiana courts. In the meantime, Ryan attended school through a phone hookup. He also became a celebrity. Through his story, people learned a great deal about AIDS, its causes, and how it spreads. In 1985, the Whites won their court case.

Ryan White outlived his diagnosis by more than five years. During that time he became an inspiring activist and passionate public advocate for children with AIDS. His efforts helped destigmatize a cruel illness and fundamentally altered the course of AIDS research.

Ryan died on April 8, 1990, one month shy of high-school graduation. Four months later, Congress passed the Ryan White CARE Act. It remains the nation's largest provider of services for people living with AIDS.

Tokata Iron Eyes

Tokata Iron Eyes, a Lakota Sioux youth activist, was born in 2003 and grew up on the Standing Rock reservation in North Dakota. In 2016, when Energy Transfer Partners announced that it had permits to build the Dakota Access Pipeline through the Missouri River, on her tribe's sacred land and its only water source, she and fellow tribal youth launched the Rezpect Our Water campaign. Their actions started a movement that brought thousands to the protests camps in Standing Rock and made headlines internationally.

In my fourteen years of life, I've asked myself many times why humans are so filled with hatred and anger. I've come to a conclusion that it is because we are also filled with hurt. I grew up on the Standing Rock reservation, a remote and rural place, and from a young age, I observed cycles of hurt everywhere I went. It was in my uncles showing up drunk or high on holidays. It was in my aunt asking me, only ten years old, for money so she could go feed her addiction instead of feeding her kids. And it was in the depression that I saw so many of my peers going through. I used to think this cycle was only on the reservation, that it was only affecting my family, my people, and so I blamed them.

In April 2016, I helped start a movement against the Dakota Access Pipeline. It was set to go straight through sacred sites that were thousands of years old. They were the burial grounds of my ancestors. It was also going through the Standing Rock Sioux tribe's only source of fresh water, the Missouri River. I couldn't just sit and watch. Instead I helped make a video with the Rezpect Our Water campaign that got the attention of millions of people. The youth of Standing Rock delivered a petition to Washington, DC, on foot, which made people want to stand up even more. And so, in August, a protest camp began in my homelands. The Oceti Sakowin protest camp held more than ten thousand people at its peak. That's ten thousand people whom I was able to learn from.

And here's what I discovered:

This cycle of hurt that I've spoken of hasn't just affected my people—it has affected everyone. Whether we realize it or not, we were all colonized. At some point

in time, we all lived in harmony with the earth. But we destroyed that, and then we continued to destroy each other. The trauma of being stripped of our connection with our Mother Earth has caused generations of people to blindly follow a system of hurt. The oppressed becoming the oppressors. But I'm not writing this because I want to repeat the past. I'm writing as a member of the seventh generation who believes that we can teach each other love and respect instead of hurt and anger. We can turn negative feelings into positive change. We must stay in a mind-set of compassion.

It's hard to do. When my people were standing on the front lines getting sprayed with water cannons by the police, I didn't want to have compassion. But I wasn't fighting for just my water. Those police have children who will drink from the same streams I fought for. We must teach this sort of compassion to our children and to everyone around us. By incorporating these values into our lives, we will empower others to do the same. Together we will heal, and together we will make change.

I know some people reading this are probably wondering why I'm using the movement of Standing Rock as a source of guidance since, in the end, the pipeline was still put through. I'm doing it because Standing Rock is not over. There are fights for clean water and for indigenous and human rights everywhere. We need to stay woke, especially now with a sorry excuse of a president. We can't sit back down. If anything, we need to stand up taller than before. I am fourteen years old and I already know that I will fight this fight until I can guarantee a future with fresh water and clean skies for my children.

THE WHAT
· · · · · · · · · · · · · · · ·

"Show up, dive in, stay at it."

That's some dang good advice on how to be an effective activist from our forty-fourth president, Barack Obama. But what, exactly, are you going to be an activist for? Which issue gets your heart beating? Maybe there are a bunch of problems you'd like to help fix. Maybe just one. Or maybe you don't know. You need some time to consider your options! In this section, we take a deep dive into six issues we think are important and believe you might be interested in as well: climate change, immigration, LGBTQIA rights, racial justice, religious understanding, and women's rights. We have to confess, this was tricky for us. There are topics we care a lot about—animal rights and gun control, for instance—that you won't find here. And there are others—like disability rights—that we wish we could have made more space for. Likewise, this is a book that, as the title suggests, focuses on the challenges our nation currently faces. And so our intel has a distinctly American bent. Still, we think you can apply much of what you learn here to other topics and to international problems.

We hope you will. It's a big world out there, and there's so much to do!

CLIMATE CHANGE

> "Global warming is no longer a philosophical threat, no longer a future threat, no longer a threat at all. It's our reality."
>
> —Bill McKibben, environmentalist, cofounder of 350.org

Remember the story of Chicken Little? While eating her lunch one day, Chicken Little is struck on the head by an acorn. "Oh no!" she shouts. "The sky is falling!" And then she races off to tell the king. Along the road, she runs into Ducky Lucky, Goosey Loosey, Turkey Lurkey, and every other bird in the land. Each time she sounds the same alarm. "The sky is falling! The sky is falling!" Finally, the whole panicked crew meets up with Foxy Loxy, who offers them shelter in his lair.

But hold on here. This story has a bunch of different endings.

In one version, Foxy Loxy gets everyone into his lair and eats them. In another, Cocky Locky lives long enough to warn Chicken Little and she gets away unharmed. In yet another, the sky actually *does* fall, flattening Foxy Loxy. And, in the happiest of endings, everyone escapes and they all make it to tell the king.

Well, guess what? The sky actually *is* falling. And the Chicken Littles of the world, otherwise known as scientists, have been trying to tell us this for more than fifty years. Human-induced climate change is the single most serious threat we face. And it's also the most evenhanded. Global warming doesn't recognize national borders, your gender identity, or your religion. It will ruin this beautiful planet, and every person and beast on it.

Unless we pick a different ending.

It's probably going to take all the birds in the yard. But, together, we can change the direction this story is heading. Our lives depend on it.

WHAT WE TALK ABOUT WHEN WE TALK ABOUT CLIMATE CHANGE

→ CHALLENGES

AIR POLLUTION

There are a lot of different kinds of air pollution: smog billowing out of factory smokestacks and coal plants, burning jet fuel and gasoline fumes, or agriculturally produced methane. All of them are health hazards that also accelerate climate change.

ENVIRONMENTAL RACISM

Marginalized and poor communities are often subjected to serious environmental hazards, such as toxic mining, polluted natural resources, or various other violations of their rights, because they, as a group, are devalued by society or considered powerless.

EXTREME WEATHER

Hurricanes, tornadoes, droughts, wildfires, floods, tsunamis, earthquakes—all bad things, right? And all things that are getting more and more common around the world because global warming is causing more extreme weather. It's important to recognize that the people most vulnerable to these natural disasters are poor people and people of color—people who don't have the infrastructure to protect them.

EXTINCTION

Hey, good news, we're in the sixth great mass extinction! Oh wait, no, that's terrible news. The first five, each of which wiped out at least half of all species, happened millions and millions of years ago. They were all the result of stuff like meteors, volcanoes, and sea-level falls. This sixth one is fueled by—you guessed it—human-induced climate change.

FOSSIL FUELS

Fossil fuels—coal, petroleum, natural gas, etc.—are not renewable resources. There's a limited amount and we're running out. So the energy industry has resorted to riskier and riskier methods for getting the stuff out of the ground, like offshore oil drilling, tar sands mining, and hydraulic fracturing (or *fracking*), that often result in environmental messes. For example: fracking is the process of pumping high-pressure liquid chemicals into the ground to create fractures in solid rock and release oil and natural gas. It can also poison water sources and create earthquakes. Another problem with fossil fuels is that burning them results in the emission of greenhouse gases. These gases trap heat in the atmosphere and contribute to global warming.

INDUSTRIAL FARMING

Whether or not you're an animal lover, whether or not you feel strongly about people eating animals, one thing is for sure: industrial farming is bad for the environment. It produces 37 percent of global emissions of methane, a greenhouse gas that is twenty times worse for global warming than carbon dioxide (CO_2); drives deforestation and depletes soil; and creates giant lagoons of animal waste that emit noxious gases and contaminate water supplies, among other harmful things.

MELTING ICE CAPS AND RISING OCEANS

Global warming, driven by the burning of fossil fuels, is causing ice caps to melt, which is causing sea levels to rise, completely screwing up global weather patterns and putting coastal areas in severe danger of serious flooding—like New York City, Miami, and Los Angeles, not to mention islands around the world that may one day be underwater. And in case you're wondering about the so-called debate on climate change, there really is none. According to NASA, "97 percent or more of actively publishing climate scientists agree: Climate-warming trends over the past century are extremely likely due to human activities."

NUCLEAR WASTE

Nuclear power is often promoted as a clean and cost-effective form of energy. But it's also super risky. Nuclear power plants break down, and when they do, they can cause dangerous leaks of radiation and carcinogenic waste. For instance, in 2011, a nuclear plant in Fukushima, Japan, was damaged by an earthquake-produced tsunami, unleashing terrific amounts of radioactive waste. It's been leaking ever since.

Mining for the uranium and plutonium necessary to create nuclear power and weapons is also highly problematic. In the mid- to late twentieth century, uranium mining on Native American land resulted in radiation poisoning, respiratory illness, and cancer among indigenous populations, and some of that land is still contaminated.

TOXIC WASTE

There are many kinds of toxic waste. Arsenic from electrical circuits, asbestos from building materials, cyanide from pesticides, lead from batteries and paint. Every day we dispose of things, from household cleaners to cell phones, that are not biodegradable. So they just stick around, seeping chemicals into the soil, water, and air. These chemicals have been proven to cause serious harm to the human body, from respiratory illnesses to cancer.

→WHAT WE CAN DO

IN SCHOOL

Help your school go green: Start a recycling program. Or call for an eco-challenge of new green ideas. Or shoot a video that inspires (or downright scares) your peers into doing what's right.

Plant a garden: Learning to grow fruits and vegetables at school is a proven route to a lifetime of healthier, smarter, more environmentally friendly eating. Check out organizations like kidsgardening.org, wholekidsfoundation.org, or edibleschoolyard.org for tips and tools to get growing.

Don't buy bottled water: A decent thermal flask in your backpack will last all day, and keep your water cold, too!

OUT OF SCHOOL

Be energy efficient: Turn off the lights when you leave the house, shut down your computer, encourage your parents to purchase smart appliances and fuel-efficient cars if they can, or take public transit.

Change how you eat: If and when it's possible, eat local and sustainable food, grow your own food, compost, and consider eliminating beef from your diet. If we ate beans instead of beef, we could get 75 percent of the way to the emissions reduction goal President Obama had set for the year 2025. (Trump's policies, however, are changing that goal.)

Support wildlife habitats: Make a contribution to organizations like the Nature Conservancy, the Sierra Club, or the Sea Shepherd Conservation Society.

Consider renewable energy: We can support clean energy sources like solar, wind, and geothermal through activism and education.

Support legislation: There are always environmentally friendly initiatives being put before your elected representatives. Keep yourself informed and let them know how you feel.

Offset your carbon footprint: Websites like carbonfootprint.com or climatecare.org will help you calculate your carbon footprint and offset your negative impact by contributing to global environmental projects. If you can engage your parents, or whoever makes the financial decisions in your house, even better!

WE HAVE SOME QUESTIONS
FOR GAVIN SCHMIDT, NASA

Gavin Schmidt is a climate scientist and the director of the Goddard Institute for Space Studies at NASA. He is an expert at climate modeling, which is making computer simulations of Earth's climate to help understand its present health and the outlook for its future.

What are the biggest contributors to global warming?

There is human versus natural warming. Right now the issue is 100 percent human contribution. That means the things we put into the atmosphere, the worst of which is carbon dioxide. Carbon dioxide comes from the burning of fossil fuels like coal, and [from] deforestation.

Why do climate change deniers say there's no hard science or the science is fuzzy?

What people say is not always true. And people don't like to believe that what they do contributes to ruining the planet.

Why aren't people marching in the street the way they do for other atrocities like war and police brutality?

Climate change is a global problem, but we don't see it locally so much. And carbon dioxide is invisible. Also, global warming is a slow process. If you break your arm, you have an emergency and so you go to the hospital. But if you have diabetes or high blood pressure, you may not realize it and therefore don't treat them properly. That doesn't mean these diseases are less serious than a broken arm. But they're a slower, less visible situation. Our brains deal with these things differently. We see the cost of not using fossil fuels, but we don't see the cost of using them.

What does it mean that the United States has pulled out of the Paris Climate Agreement?

The Paris Agreement [came out of] a conference [in 2015] in which 195 countries agreed to try to lower carbon emissions. The idea was for everyone to sign on so no one [country] would be disadvantaged by sacrifices or choices. It was the most successful negotiation ever.

There were no specific rules, but the idea was to get together every few years and see what works, what doesn't, to bring new ideas and share intelligence. The United States pulling out is perplexing and counterproductive, but is in the end not going to have that big an effect. Renewables [like water, wind, and solar power] are becoming cheaper anyway.

Is there hope?

Yes. Lots. DC may be experiencing gridlock but lots of good things are happening.

There is innovation and new technology and conscious planning to reduce emissions. Companies are retrofitting old buildings to make them more energy efficient. States are investing in wind and solar power and geothermal power. Cities from New York to Burlington to Sacramento are getting together to look at how to make transportation and other services more efficient. There is lots of sensible planning going on. Things can and will get better. There is hope!

Spotlight on
Our Children's Trust

Levi Draheim lives by the ocean in central Florida. He loves his home and thinks of the beach as "another mother." But every time a big storm hits, the neighborhood loses another section of dune. Levi knows that the rising seas and unstable weather are a direct result of climate change, and that irresponsible environmental policy is contributing to that change. So he's suing the federal government.

Levi is ten years old. And he is not alone.

Supported by the Oregon-based environmental organization Our Children's Trust (OCT), twenty-one young Americans are engaged in a landmark lawsuit over their constitutional right to a stable climate system. If they succeed, it will mark a turning point in the long battle to protect our country's natural resources. And it all began at the movies.

OCT's founder, Julia Olson, is an experienced environmental lawyer who was working on cases impacting the rivers and forests and wildlife throughout the Pacific Northwest. Eight months pregnant with her second child, she slipped into the cool of a movie theater in August 2006 to watch the Al Gore documentary *An Inconvenient Truth*. She was stunned by what she saw, cried through much of the film, and emerged determined to focus her energies on the climate crisis.

Around the same time, Mary Wood, a professor at the University of Oregon School of Law, was developing an argument involving the public trust doctrine, which holds that essential natural resources must be preserved for the benefit of present and future generations alike. Professor Wood reasoned that the atmosphere must be preserved as part of the public trust. Olson and Wood soon joined forces and consulted Professor James

ALEXANDRA STYRON

Hansen, the scientist widely considered the "father of climate change awareness." Combining their knowledge of law, theory, and science, the three swung into action.

On Mother's Day 2011, Our Children's Trust supported fifty climate recovery legal actions on behalf of youth throughout the United States. Since that time, OCT has supported additional actions in the United States and around the globe. OCT has also developed a unique program, Youth Climate Action Now (YouCAN), that supports grassroots efforts encouraging US towns and cities to adopt science-based climate recovery ordinances.

The federal case in which Levi and his friends are plaintiffs presents an exciting new frontier. For years, studies have shown that the maximum safe level of carbon dioxide in our atmosphere is 350 parts per million (meaning, for every million air particles, 350 of them are CO_2). In March 2016, the world went well beyond that safe level when CO_2 levels passed 400 parts per million (ppm). And while many other large countries have been notorious environmental offenders, a disproportionate amount of the junk we breathe is produced right here at home, where the United States has, over time, emitted more carbon dioxide into our atmosphere than any other country.

"The US is responsible for more than twenty-five percent of global emissions on the planet," explains OCT deputy director Lou Helmuth. "But we're not twenty-five percent of the land mass, and we're not twenty-five percent of the population. We have an obligation not only to bring CO_2 levels down on a national level, but state by state as well." OCT argues that, by allowing carbon dioxide levels to rise to over 400 ppm, the federal government is violating the plaintiffs' constitutional rights to a climate system capable of sustaining human life.

If the case holds, the US government will be forced to implement a detailed climate recovery plan to reduce CO_2 concentrations back down to below 350 ppm. "Nobody has taken such a systemic approach before," says Helmuth, expressing pride in the ingenuity of the action. But if Helmuth is eager to highlight the merits of the argument, he reserves his highest praise for the kids involved. "They came to us," he explains of the plaintiffs and their willingness to sign on. It is, he says "the clarity of the lens through which they see human relationships" that will make them successful in the work they're doing.

Having fended off multiple attempts to have the case dismissed, Levi Draheim and the other young plaintiffs have now won a decision by the Ninth Circuit Court of Appeals that will allow their case to proceed to trial. And hopefully, after that, it will be on to the Supreme Court.

Spotlight on
Boyan Slat and the Ocean Cleanup

If you've ever been lucky enough to go deep-sea diving, you know how beautiful it is down there. You might spot colorful fish, coral like great castles, exotic sea plants, and maybe a spiny thing or two you can't even identify. But what sixteen-year-old Boyan Slat found when he went diving off the coast of Greece in 2011 was a different kind of creature altogether: plastic. Gobs and gobs of plastic. More plastic than fish. It bummed him out, and it got him thinking. Back in the Netherlands, he noticed that everybody, even grown-ups, threw plastic into the waterways. It was just the sort of carelessness that created the Great Pacific Garbage Patch, a massive area of swirling marine debris discovered in the 1980s, made of billions of pieces of plastic. (And that's just a fraction of the estimated five trillion pieces of plastic that litter Earth's great bodies of water!)

Boyan has always loved tinkering and making things. So he got to work on an idea for cleaning the ocean. He began working on a barrier designed to collect garbage in the water, separating waste from vital plankton and other sea life. In 2013, Boyan founded his company, the Ocean Cleanup. His machine has gone through hundreds of changes in the last few years. It now involves a series of booms that fan out across the ocean, helping to feed the plastic into a central area where it will be collected by boats.

To date, the Ocean Cleanup company has raised more than $30 million from philanthropists and investors. Boyan has been hailed as a visionary and hero for the planet. In 2014, the UN Environment Programme gave him their Champions of the Earth award. *Forbes* magazine included him in its "30 Under 30" list in 2016; in 2017, *Reader's Digest* named him European of the Year.

ALEXANDRA STYRON

WE HAVE SOME QUESTIONS FOR SHAILENE WOODLEY

In 2011, Shailene Woodley had a breakout role in *The Descendants* with George Clooney, soon followed by starring roles in the Divergent series, *The Fault in Our Stars*, *Snowden*, and HBO's *Big Little Lies*. In 2015, Shailene joined the struggle to protect Mauna Kea, a mountain sacred to Hawaii's indigenous people, from the construction of an eighteen-story telescope. A year later, she stood in solidarity with the Lakota Sioux of Standing Rock against the Dakota Access Pipeline, eventually getting arrested for the cause. Shailene is a cofounder of the youth leadership nonprofit All It Takes and sits on the board of the voter empowerment organization Our Revolution.

Many of the movements you've been a part of are not simply environmental movements but specifically struggles against environmental racism. What do you see your role as a white person being in this work?

There are thousands of privileges that add to my daily comfort and existence because I am white. Simply put: there are doubts, fears, discriminations, and anxieties that I will never know, because I am white. There are possibilities, opportunities, circumstances that will expand my reality, each and every day, because I am white. My personal belief is that until the day comes when my Native American sister, and my African American brother, and my Muslim mentor, and my Indian friend thrive in a landscape that caters to their needs at the same rate as my own, I, as a white individual, am, simply by existing, contributing to a system that is racist, oppressive, and manipulated to keep it that way.

So how do we change this? We talk. We communicate. We support. We acknowledge. We humble ourselves. We ask questions. We listen. We get a bit uncomfortable. We let go of our desire to be right, and replace it with our desire to collectively heal and thrive. And then, we take action. Real action. And real action means letting go of all attachments to what you thought you once knew, and being open to all that you have yet to learn. Standing Rock, for me, was a beautiful example of this. I believe, more than anything, my role in that movement was simply speaking about it to other white people. Asking questions that I myself had never once asked, and seeking space for offering support to a community that needed it. Standing Rock was a movement led by Native Americans. My role was to open up dialogues amidst white communities about why and how this pipeline movement even existed.

It may seem impossible to address the systemic disorders that exist in our nation. It may seem out of our hands, too big to tackle. But it is not. It starts by first acknowledging the privilege white individuals have, and then offering the use and the megaphone of that privilege to communities that need it to make a difference in their lives. Standing Rock, Black Lives Matter, LGBTQIA equality—these movements are not movements for me to be a spokesperson of. They are movements that I can offer my body to, my support to, my ears to, and my heart to. The platform and protection my skin color grant me can be a platform and a tool for those who are not given the same security by our nation. A hero complex will not solve anything, but a humble desire to support will.

You split your time between acting and activism. What recommendations do you have for young activists trying to manage their time and responsibilities?

I believe that the word activist simply means: being a good human being. That's it. A person who practices empathy, compassion, positive growth and expansion, and love. I've come to realize that there is no division between where and how I spend my time. I choose to be an activist—a good human being—every day.

I think it is too easy to get lost in the excitement and sexiness of protests and the big, loud aspects of movements. Though [it is] vital for revolution, often we pay more attention to that side of activism and forget the smaller but equally as important side of it: showing up for others and supporting one another on an individual basis. Our world is starving for love. Don't ever forget that even if no one is watching, or you can't Instagram it, or you gain zero recognition or attention for it, any moment spent with love and compassion with another individual is just as vital to the progression of our planet as a petition, or a protest, or a strike. You never know what seeds will be planted, and what healing will take place from any given interaction. So, I suppose my advice to those of you out there who may be struggling with how to lead an independently fruitful, passionate life while also wanting to be an active participant in social and planetary growth is: take the pressure off of yourself. Know that you will end up being exactly where you are needed, when you are needed, in a public way. And in a private way, dedicate your life to that of goodness. In order to change the world, we must know what the world needs. And in order to know what the world needs, we must displace our egos, observe, and listen to voices that need an ear. And finally, take time to enjoy life. If you are burnt out, driven by guilt, exhausted, and overworked, chances are your flame won't be burning as brightly and as powerfully as if you are energetically full.

How did you first learn about the causes you're involved in and realize that you wanted to be involved?

For me, it all began with trees. Ever since I was a little girl, I was obsessed with nature—I felt as if it spoke to me, grounded me, cradled me. I was more comfortable being outside than inside, and more eager to hang with the crooked branches at our local park than I was with other people. I think having that relationship with nature opened my eyes to how much we as human beings were doing to destroy our sacred Mother Earth. Then 9/11 happened. I was in fifth grade. I remember that was the moment I realized how lucky I was to have two loving parents, a healthy younger brother, and a safe home to live in. It was that moment that I began to notice my innate privilege. My obsession with empathy was a result of 9/11 and the fact that both of my parents are psychologists. Although [they] would never share confidential names, [they] would share stories with me about what they witnessed working as counselors and therapists in local public schools. The hardships and the struggles that so many kids my own age went through blew my young mind. It immediately made me yearn to be as compassionate and as helpful as possible, in all ways.

IMMIGRATION

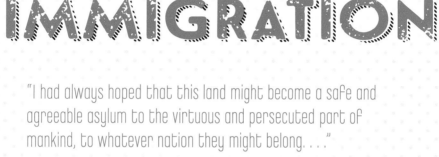

"I had always hoped that this land might become a safe and agreeable asylum to the virtuous and persecuted part of mankind, to whatever nation they might belong. . . ."

—George Washington, First US president

The United States, in all its complex glory, was created as a society of immigrants. The Founding Fathers recognized that different kinds of people have different gifts, and that pluralism would be the nation's strength. It would also discourage tyranny. As James Madison, a congressional delegate, primary contributor to the US Constitution, and future president put it, "[W]here there is such a variety of sects, there cannot be a majority of any one sect to oppress and persecute the rest."

OK, well, that didn't exactly work out. In the last 250 years, some sects—groups bound by their beliefs—have done a pretty bang-up job of oppressing other sects. Still, one thing remains true. The extraordinary diversity of our population is what makes America unique, and it's what makes us strong. Every nationality, ethnicity, and tribe has contributed particular knowledge, traditions, perspective, and skills. And together, we've built one of the greatest nations in human history.

We've also been measured by our compassion. Long before the Statue of Liberty appeared and Emma Lazarus's famous lines "Give me your tired, your poor, your huddled masses yearning to breathe free" were engraved there, America was a haven for refugees, people fleeing war, famine, and religious or political persecution.

But that doesn't mean immigration isn't complicated. Sometimes it seems like much of the world is in flames. There are so many people seeking asylum in the United States. Can we welcome them all? If not, then who *should* we take? And what about the others? What is wise? What is humane? And just what is it that defines us as "Americans"?

WHAT WE TALK ABOUT WHEN WE TALK ABOUT IMMIGRATION

→ CHALLENGES

BARRIERS TO CITIZENSHIP

Of the more than 13 million legal permanent residents currently in the US, the Department of Homeland Security estimates that 8.8 million are eligible to become citizens. But those who want to often face obstacles. The cost of a naturalization application is over $700—way too high for many people. (And that's assuming you've been able to obtain a "green card" conferring legal status.) Language is also a barrier: you have to pass English and civics exams to become a citizen. These take time and access that poor people don't always have. So basically, it's harder for lower-income people to become citizens.

DENIAL OF DUE PROCESS RIGHTS

The Fifth and Fourteenth Amendments to the Constitution both have due process clauses. This guarantees the right to a fair, speedy, orderly trial, and protects people from punishment before they've had that just legal treatment. But frequently, people detained at the border by Immigration and Customs Enforcement (ICE) are denied these due process rights. They are held for long periods of time without access to a fair trial, bail, or parole.

DETENTION AND BORDER PATROL ABUSES

People who enter the United States from other countries often do so out of desperation. They may be fleeing war, famine, or extreme poverty. The journey itself may also be fraught with trouble: exposure to the elements, abuse at the hands of human traffickers, or ill treatment by border patrol officers. If they end up in detention, more misery awaits. The facilities may be dirty, crowded, short on food, and lacking proper mental health or medical treatment. Physical and sexual abuse are common.

DEPORTATION AND SEPARATION OF FAMILIES

ICE deports hundreds of thousands of undocumented immigrants every year, which means that hundreds of thousands of families are separated every year. Often, this leaves a single parent attempting to support a family on one income. In other cases, children lose both parents and are placed in foster care. All of these results have been linked to increased poverty and decreased access to education, healthcare, and food.

THREATS TO DACA

Signed into law by President Obama in 2012, Deferred Action for Childhood Arrivals (DACA) was designed to help people who were brought to the United States illegally as young children stay in the country. If they met the requirements, they could live and work here legally, free from threat of detainment and deportation. They could request renewal of this freedom every two years. The Trump administration opposes DACA and has threatened to deport recipients.

TREATMENT OF REFUGEES

In 2017, President Trump's Executive Order 13769, also known as the "Muslim ban," attempted to bar travel from Syria, Yemen, Somalia, Sudan, Libya, Iran, and Iraq to the United States for 90 days, halt resettlement of refugees for 120 days, and prohibit Syrian refugees indefinitely, a violation of UN refugee relocation agreements. Terrorism was the justification for this ban, but the people affected most were families: grandparents, grandchildren, nieces, uncles, in-laws, anyone beyond the nuclear family. In a period of global refugee crises due to war and climate disaster, this ban, its redrafts, and the ideology behind it are particularly concerning.

XENOPHOBIA

One of the elements at the core of all these issues, be it restrictions against Mexicans and Latin Americans, or Haitians, or people from majority Muslim

countries, is *xenophobia*, a fear of or prejudice against foreign people. When people feel stressed about their own circumstances, they often express a kind of tribalism. Groups will band together and pull up the drawbridge against other groups who might threaten their resources. This can lead to bigotry, discrimination, and violence against people who seem "different."

→ WHAT WE CAN DO

IN SCHOOL

Fight to keep ICE out of your school: Mayors, legislators, and school officials in some parts of the country have moved to keep ICE from entering schools. Ask your school administration what they're doing to protect immigrant students. Demand that they address the issue.

Raise awareness: Make "know your rights" materials available to immigrant students. Schedule a teach-in to educate nonimmigrants about how to assist the immigrant population. Don't forget to invite parents, teachers, and staff!

OUT OF SCHOOL

Advocate for legislation: Get in touch with your representatives and urge them to defend DACA, support refugee assistance programs, and fight deportation policies that separate immigrant families.

Organize a fundraiser: Engage with groups like United We Dream, Families for Freedom, the Immigrant Defense Project, the International Rescue Committee, or immigrant rights organizations in your area.

Spotlight on
United We Dream

These days, when we talk about immigration reform, we are often talking about Dreamers.

Named for the legislation they have fought to get passed for years—the Development, Relief, and Education for Alien Minors Act—Dreamers represent one of the most powerful youth movements in America today. They are fighting for their very lives, and for one of the bedrock principles of our country: that we are a nation of immigrants.

The Constitution, BTW, establishes the right to life, liberty, and property for all people, not just citizens.

The Dream, such as it is, started with the new millennium. That's when the first effort began to create a path to citizenship for the nearly two million immigrants living in the United States who had been brought here as children. Without a viable way to become legal, these people would continue to live in constant fear of deportation. If they were kicked out, many of them would be going back to countries they didn't even remember.

From the very start, student groups were a huge part of the Dreamer campaign. They pushed hard for legislation and, in 2001, the first bill, focused on educational advancement, was introduced in Congress. This bill was followed by subsequent ones in the House and the Senate, sponsored by Democrats and Republicans alike. But the issue was a political hot potato. Each time, the DREAM bill failed to get the requisite votes.

Finally, in 2007, when a bipartisan version of the DREAM Act failed to pass in the Senate, youth organizers nationwide decided to consolidate their efforts. In 2008, with the help of the National Immigration Law Center, they founded United We Dream (UWD). Their aim was to create a youth-led organization powered by the very people directly impacted by the system. United We Dream would organize, provide resources, and continue to build momentum for immigration rights. UWD soon became the largest youth-led immigration organization in the country.

And they got stuff done. In 2012, thanks in part to pressure from UWD, President Obama enacted DACA. Nearly one million Dreamers signed up for the program. Shortly thereafter, UWD launched their We Can't Wait campaign to halt deportations and family separation in the rest of the undocumented community. Besides political campaigns, UWD has helped legions of Dreamers enroll in college, obtain driver's licenses, understand their rights, and get legal help.

In the end, the DACA program remains the most important safety net for Dreamers. And it has also proved to be the most fragile. When President Obama tried to expand the program in 2014, twenty-six states (all but two of which had Republican governors) sued the courts to bring it to an end. Those efforts failed. But in September 2017, President Trump rescinded the program and challenged Congress to come up with something else. It was a move that solved no problems and offered no solutions—but left thousands of young people living in fear, with little idea of what their future would hold.

The work of United We Dream continues on, never more urgent than it is today.

Some Numbers on Dreamers

1.3 million: Number of immigrants currently eligible for DACA (the Migration Policy Institute)

800,000: Number of DACA recipients, approximately (United States Citizenship and Immigration Services)

6.5 years old: Average age of DACA recipient when they came to the United States (Center for American Progress 2017 survey)

Under 31: Age you must have been in 2012 in order to apply for DACA (US Citizenship and Immigration Services)

700,000: Number of people who would lose their jobs without DACA (*Newsweek*)

$400 billion: Money the economy would lose without DACA in the next ten years (Center for American Progress)

72%: Dreamers who are getting or have gotten higher education (Center for American Progress)

1,800+: Number of governors, attorneys general, state representatives, judges, and other leaders who have written in support of Dreamers (withdreamers.com)

8 out of 10: Number of American voters who support DACA (ABC News/*Washington Post* poll)

WE HAVE SOME QUESTIONS FOR
JOSE ANTONIO VARGAS, DEFINE AMERICAN

Jose Antonio Vargas is a Pulitzer Prize–winning journalist, filmmaker, and entrepreneur. He is the founder of the media and culture organization Define American and editor of the documentary storytelling platform #EmergingUS. In 2011, Vargas revealed his undocumented immigration status in an article in *The New York Times Magazine*. He went on to write, produce, and direct the autobiographical documentary *Documented*, and also directed MTV's *White People*.

Did you always know you wanted to be a writer? Did you have any sense that your personal story might lead you to political activism?

I found out that I was undocumented at sixteen, when I tried to get a driver's license; after that my world changed. As far as the US government went, I didn't exist.

To me, writing was a way of showing America I deserved to be here. The work of people like James Baldwin and Toni Morrison, who live at the intersection of issues and the human experience, taught me that I wanted to be someone who could capture the world we live in now, in all its complexity. Developing my own identity when I felt like I fit into so many categories and was left out of others—like being an "American," for instance—was a challenge, and I think that's why in my writing I seek to disrupt and transcend binary, simplistic ways of looking at the world.

First and foremost, I'm a journalist. What's been interesting is how the word "activist" is used to discredit journalistic objectivity. For example, I realized that immigration is maybe the least understood (yet most politicized) issue of our time, so—I started Define American to help tell the stories that weren't being told by the media. Now I am considered an "activist." To me, that is intentional and deliberate. We've been programmed to believe that the default voice is that of the straight white male. The truth is that everyone comes with a point of view and brings something to the table. Ethically as journalists, we learn where those lines are and monitor ourselves.

For many activists, their role in the social justice movement is preceded by "coming out"—as gay, as a rape survivor, as a woman who has had an abortion. In 2011, you "came out" as undocumented, which put you at real risk. Can you talk about this decision?

Coming out as undocumented was one of the scariest decisions I've ever made, and yet it was also one of the easiest. I had to do it. I couldn't sit idly by while I saw more and more undocumented young people come out online and organize in person. I came out as gay first. At that time I'd recently found out I was undocumented and I knew I had to choose a closet to come out of, so one day at school I decided to raise my hand and tell my classmates I was gay.

When [as an adult] I came out as undocumented, I was prepared for the worst. I had to be. Luckily, that didn't happen, but my life did change in a lot of ways, both bad and good. I knew that I wanted to start Define American so that we could facilitate the conversation around immigration that I didn't feel was happening at the time. We were hearing political jargon on the news and forgetting that we were talking about people's lives. I felt like I was in a unique position as a professional journalist to bring some of those people's stories to the surface, so that Americans could see what—and who—we're really talking about when we talk about immigration.

Statistics show that immigrants have an overwhelmingly positive effect on American society. They are more likely than native-born citizens to start and own businesses. They contribute billions of dollars in taxes every year, and almost 30 percent of immigrants go to college. Also, contrary to the current administration's many comments,

immigrants commit fewer crimes and are incarcerated at
much lower rates than US citizens. So why do you think
this message that immigrants are a huge problem gets so
much traction?

Historically, politicians have always teased out and exploited latent xenophobia
in order to control people. It's a tactic. As we've seen with this last election, facts
have gone out the window. At Define American we launched an initiative called
#FactsMatter, which we share with media organizations, educators, and other people
looking for information about the basic facts of immigration that are always reported
wrong or left out of the narrative. The truth is that the problems in our country are
layered and can't be attributed to just one or two demographic groups. But people
want a clear place to put their blame and anger. Immigrants always end up being the
scapegoats, because we're looked at as outsiders.

Since 2012, nearly 800,000 people have signed up for the
DACA program. In doing so, they trusted the government
with their private information. Now that DACA is under
threat, the government has all the details they need to
find people and deport them. What can be done to protect
these people?

When DACA was first announced by President Obama in 2012, there was a lot of
concern about what would happen if the DACA database was used against applicants,
or if it got into the wrong hands. Now it's in the wrong hands. We're all at risk. It's
been encouraging to see how many people spoke up to defend DACA when Attorney
General Jeff Sessions announced that President Trump was planning to end the
program. We need people to keep speaking up and keep looking for ways to help their
undocumented friends and neighbors in their own communities.

You founded an organization called Define American. What
do you think defines a person as American?

I think one of the most polarizing realities in our country right now is that everybody
has a different idea of what it means to be an American. To me, living in a

place where it's OK to have different opinions and to be able to talk about them constructively is what makes America great. I'm focused on the fact that we can have the conversation; others are focused on the outcome of the conversation itself. America stops becoming America when we no longer have the right to define America for ourselves. Good citizenship, not in papers, but in action, means to show our love for our country by fulfilling our own potential in its service and in the service of our communities. That, to me, defines American.

Spotlight on
PROOF: Media for Social Justice

Founded by photojournalist Leora Kahn, PROOF: Media for Social Justice is a nonprofit organization based in New York City that uses visual storytelling and education to inspire action on human rights and to create attitude and policy change. Their "Picture Justice" is a program that educates high-school students on social justice issues and empowers them through photojournalism.

In 2017, PROOF partnered with the United Nations International School (UNIS) in New York City. UNIS students focused on the stories of undocumented immigrants. The result was a large-scale exhibition titled *(un)DOCUMENTED*. Many of the participants were transformed by the experience.

Here are a couple of the young people they trained their lenses on:

ISRAT

"Being undocumented and Muslim, there are layers of oppression and stress. You have to deal with the stress of being undocumented; being fearful all the time; not knowing where you are going to be even the next day. And on top of that you have to be afraid or vigilant when you're on the streets. Especially if

you are a visible Muslim; if you have a beard; if you're hijabi. If you look Muslim, there is that double layer of 'be careful.'

"As soon as something happens, my first thought is 'omg I hope this person is not Muslim' and my second thought is 'damn I have to stand up for my religion again.' I'm tired of doing that and I feel like I shouldn't have to do that because I'm a part of American society as much as the next person."

—Israt immigrated with her family from Bangladesh to the United States at age six. They arrived in 2001, five months before the 9/11 attacks.

I have a humanity, and that all people every-where deserve rights."

—Abraham is an Eritrean refugee born in Sudan who came to the United States when he was nine months old. He is the former executive director of Families for Freedom, a multiethnic human rights organization in New York for families facing and fighting deportation.

ABRAHAM

"I was walking home from work a couple years ago and I got picked up for a robbery that happened on my block. Physically I couldn't have done it, but I ended up on Rikers Island [jail]. I had convictions during the War on Drugs in the nineties, but since then I've gone to college and grad school. I was able to get bond. Upon my release from Rikers, I went to ten immigrant rights organizations and basically they were like, 'You have a criminal conviction, so we cannot help you.'

"What I went through is a human rights issue and not just an immigrant issue; the fact that I'm a human being, I have a family,

go to PROOF.org and learn how you can bring a program like it to your school!

Lisette Diaz

Lisette Diaz was born in 1993 in Santiago, Chile. She moved to the United States at age six and has lived in New York since she arrived. A 2016 graduate of Harvard University, Lisette currently works as a paralegal at the American Civil Liberties Union in the Immigrants' Rights Project. She plans to attend law school and make a career out of helping other immigrants.

I came to this country in 2000, when I was six years old. Back then I didn't think about borders, I didn't think about breaking the law or about what it would mean to be undocumented. I thought about my dad. The year before, he had left Chile and come to the United States to look for work. My mom and I stayed back because we could only afford one plane ticket. Even then we had to sell almost all of the furniture in my grandma's house. A few months after my dad left, my mom found me crying underneath a table at my cousin's birthday party. I kept asking her why everyone else had a dad but I didn't. This was the moment that broke my mom's heart and it was the moment she decided that we needed to come to the United States to reunite our family. On the twelve-hour flight, I thought about seeing my dad for the first time in over a year. I thought about being able to hug him and having my family reunited.

I don't think people realize how hard it is to leave behind everything you've ever known, to leave most of your family behind, to come to a country where you don't know anyone and where you don't speak the language. The only thing you have to hold on to is hope, so you desperately cling to it. Hope that everything will work out in the end, hope that this will be a better life, hope that you will have more opportunities.

I knew I was undocumented from a young age. But I still felt very American. I went to school, pledged allegiance to the American flag every day. All of the friends I had growing up were American and my main language became English. It wasn't until I got to high school that I really started to feel different. That's when I realized that I couldn't get a license like my friends were doing, or work like my friends were doing. I couldn't apply for financial aid to go to college like the rest of my friends.

At this moment in time, my community is under attack. It feels like every day I wake up and try to exist under the facade that everything is OK. I go to work, go to the gym, make attempts to hang out with friends. But every day there are more stories of undocumented youth being detained and in some cases deported. Every day I hear about someone else's parents being picked up. Another family shattered. But I will not give up. I have lived here for eighteen years. I have completed the entirety of my education in this country. I have built my entire life in this country. I am an undocumented American.

LGBTQIA RIGHTS

> "I didn't want to live a life without love."
>
> —Edith "Edie" Windsor, LGBTQIA activist

Progress has a funny way of sneaking up on us. People fight for years and years to obtain their rights and then victory shelves the struggle—in history books. Once upon a time, women couldn't vote. Once upon a time, black people couldn't vote. Once upon a time, black people couldn't marry white people. Heck, black and white people couldn't even sit at the same lunch counter.

You know all of this, and still it seems like the Dark Ages.

But do you realize how recent the victories are that confer some very basic rights on LGBTQIA people? They happened in *your* lifetime.

In 2010, Edie Windsor sued the United States for the right to be recognized as the legal spouse and therefore heir with full rights to the estate of her partner of forty-four years; the two women had legally married in Canada in 2007. Windsor's Supreme Court case, followed by another in 2015—Obergefell v. Hodges—cleared the way for same-sex marriage to be legalized in all fifty states. Historically speaking, that was, like, five minutes ago. And get this. As recently as 2003, the year many of you were born, you could go to jail in some states just for hooking up with someone of the same gender.

Jail!

So, yeah, things have gotten a lot better for the LGBTQIA community, and not just legally. Attitudes have changed dramatically too. Recent Pew Research polls find most Americans support same-sex marriage, with 62 percent now favoring the institution (up from 35 percent in 2001) and only 32 percent opposing. It probably won't come as any surprise to you that the generation that most strongly supports gay and transgender rights is yours (74 percent of Americans born after 1980 favor same-sex marriage). But even your grandparents' generation has gotten way cooler about marriage, adoption, and transgender rights.

Still, there's a lot of work left to be done. Discrimination in the workplace remains a troubling reality, and there are many court battles to be waged  to knock it down. There is, as well, a complicated argument being carried out around matters of faith. While some of us fight for religious freedom as an expression of what makes us a truly inclusive country, others use religion as a shield to safeguard their own bigotry, and to keep people out. We still have a long way to go before we eradicate homophobic language from our daily lives. And, as Susan Sommer, former director of Constitutional Litigation at Lambda Legal, frames it, transgender rights are the "next frontier."

WHAT WE TALK ABOUT WHEN WE TALK ABOUT LGBTQIA ISSUES

→ CHALLENGES

BATHROOM LAWS

Many states have laws that require people to use bathrooms that correspond to the sex they were assigned at birth. This is a problem for a lot of people who don't identify with their original sex assignment. It can also be genuinely dangerous—for example, forcing a trans woman to use a "male" restroom can put her in a potentially pretty scary situation.

CONVERSION THERAPY

Conversion therapy (also sometimes called "reparative therapy") is based on the idea that homosexuality is a mental disorder, one that can be "cured." Historically, these methods have included chemical castration, electric shocks to the genitals, lobotomies, and other forms of torture and mutilation. Today, conversion efforts tend to be more psychological than physical, but are still harmful. As of 2017, only nine states have banned the use of conversion therapy on minors.

DISCRIMINATION AGAINST LGBTQIA PARENTS

LGBTQIA parents often face obstacles in establishing legal parent-child relationships. *Second parent* or *coparent* adoption is the legal procedure through which same-sex parents legally establish parenthood of their child. But that

right is only guaranteed in about twenty of fifty states. In June 2017, the Supreme Court made same-sex adoption legal in every state, but some states still refuse to comply. And when it comes to custody battles, transgender parents often have their gender identity used against them.

EMPLOYMENT DISCRIMINATION

About 40 percent of gay, lesbian, and bisexual people experience harassment at their place of employment. For transgender people, that percentage is a shocking 97 percent. Trans people have an unemployment rate double that of anyone else in the country. Around one in ten LGBTQIA people have left a job because they didn't feel welcome due to their gender identity, sexual orientation, or both. A person can still legally be fired for being gay in twenty-eight states and for being transgender in thirty.

EXCLUSION FROM FAITH COMMUNITIES

Unfortunately, many faith communities discriminate against LGBTQIA people. This can often mean that families are torn apart when members choose their faith community over a LGBTQIA family member.

EXCLUSION FROM THE MILITARY

The US military's Don't Ask, Don't Tell policy, which was effectively a ban on gay and lesbian men and women serving openly in the military, was ended by President Obama in 2011. In the past few years, protections for trans people have also increased: since 2016, people cannot be discharged based on their gender identity, and as of 2017, transgender people can enlist. But these rights

are now under attack by the Trump administration, inequalities persist, and LGBTQIA people in the military are still more vulnerable to abuses.

HATE CRIMES

Hate crimes are crimes motivated by prejudice. For LGBTQIA people, this is often referred to as "queer bashing." The most common form affecting the broader LGBTQIA community today is violence against trans women of color, who are being murdered at alarming rates. In 2009, President Obama signed the Matthew Shepard and James Byrd Jr. Hate Crimes Prevention Act, which gives the government more power and funding to prosecute crimes against LGBTQIA people. But twenty states still don't have increased penalties for crimes committed against gay people and thirty-four states don't have them for crimes against trans people.

HEALTHCARE

Every community has specific healthcare needs. Historically, HIV and AIDS have struck LGBTQIA communities hardest. LGBTQIA people also have a high rate of mental health issues, and transgender people often need access to hormone replacement therapy and various gender confirmation surgeries. Unfortunately, it can be difficult for people to find LGBTQIA-friendly healthcare—care and service from a professional who recognizes them, validates them, and doesn't discriminate against them.

HOUSING DISCRIMINATION

The federal Fair Housing Act, passed in 1968, was designed to protect renters and buyers from discrimination based on race, sex, religion, or national origin. Familial status (i.e. whether or not you are in a legal union) and disability were added in 1988. You might notice a couple of missing categories—*sexual orientation* and *gender identity.* Some states have protections for LGBTQIA people seeking housing, but nearly half do not. It wasn't until 2017 that a federal judge ruled for the first time that legally, the Fair Housing Act *does* protect LGBTQIA people. This ruling doesn't mean discrimination doesn't happen—it just means it isn't legal

INCARCERATION

The incarceration rate of lesbian, gay, and bisexual people is three times that of the general adult population. One-sixth of all trans people in the United States have been to prison, and a full half of black trans people have. LGBTQIA people in prisons are more likely to face various kinds of abuse, including sexual assault. Incarcerated trans people are often deprived of essential healthcare.

MARRIAGE LAWS

Same-sex marriage was effectively legalized across all fifty states by a Supreme Court ruling in 2015. But officials in several counties in Texas and Alabama still refuse to issue marriage licenses to same-sex couples. In Mississippi, merchants maintain the right to not serve same-sex couples on "religious grounds." And conservatives all over the country continue to fight what is now the law of the land.

SUICIDE PREVENTION

The rate of suicide attempts is four times higher for LGBTQIA-identifying youth than for their straight peers. This unfortunate statistic is caused by rejection by families, bullying, and other forms of abuse—the *American Journal of Public Health* reports that every instance of abuse more than doubles the likelihood of self-harm.

YOUTH HOMELESSNESS

According to a recent University of Chicago study, 4.2 million people between the ages of 13 and 25 experience homelessness in a year. LGBTQIA youth are 120 percent more likely to be part of that group. Homelessness often occurs because of family conflict springing from a person's gender or sexuality. Homeless LGBTQIA youth have a particularly hard time finding shelter and are at a higher risk for various forms of violence.

⇒ WHAT WE CAN DO

IN SCHOOL

Join/start a Gay-Straight Alliance club (GSA): There are thousands of GSAs in middle and high schools around the country. For information on starting one at your school, head to GLSEN.org. With the help of GLSEN, you can also bring a Day of Silence or Ally Week to your school.

Campaign for gender-neutral bathrooms: Make some good trouble about this at *your* school.

OUT OF SCHOOL

Advocate for legislation: Write or call your representatives and speak your mind on the importance of anti-discrimination laws like those that prohibit hate crimes, ban conversion therapy, and support gender-neutral bathrooms.

Support organizations: check out the Trevor Project, the Audre Lorde Project, the Sylvia Rivera Law Project, Lambda Legal, FIERCE, and the American Civil Liberties Union (ACLU). You can make a donation, host a fundraiser, or organize a run/walk.

Work to make your faith community more inclusive: Is your place of worship welcoming to LGBTQIA people? Talk with your faith leaders about ways to offer support, model acceptance, and practice the true spirit of your religion.

AND EVERYWHERE

Practice respectful and inclusive language: Honor a person's gender pronoun (he, she, they, etc.). Be conscious of using gendered nouns (police officer rather than policeman, flight attendant instead of stewardess, etc.). Don't use homophobic language, and don't tolerate it from others.

WE HAVE SOME QUESTIONS FOR GAVIN GRIMM

In 2014, Gavin Grimm, a sophomore at Gloucester High School in Gloucester, Virginia, had just come out as transgender. Being a boy, he—with the school principal's permission—used the boys' bathroom. Seven weeks into the school year, some parents took issue and the school board ruled that students had to use bathrooms that aligned with the sex they were assigned at birth. Gavin fought back, taking the case to the Supreme Court, with the help of the ACLU.

There are many pressing issues affecting transgender people's lives, including some that are truly life threatening. Why do you think bathroom laws have become so important?

The people who are focusing so intensely on restrooms are doing so because it's an easy way to play on the fears of people who are uninformed about who trans people are and what our lives are like. The goal here isn't really safety. More than sixty law enforcement officials filed a brief in my case to point out that transgender people aren't a danger to anyone in public restrooms. In fact, we're more likely to be harassed, screamed at, and assaulted when we try to use public restrooms. Keeping transgender people from using public restrooms is nothing more than an attempt to eliminate transgender people from public life. Because if we can't access restrooms, we can't go to school, we can't work outside of our homes, and we can't go to healthcare facilities. Or, for that matter, libraries, shopping centers, sporting events, parks, restaurants; think of all the places where one might need a restroom break that most people take for granted. Transgender people can't leave our homes without having to carefully plan out every aspect of our day to make sure that we either don't have to go to the restroom at all or that we will have access to a safe place to go when we need it. These laws and policies are motivated by people who hope that if they don't have to see trans people like me out in the world, then we'll just go away and stop existing. And they are wrong. The conversation we should be having is about the agency of trans people, and our right to exist in the same public capacity as anyone else. To stick exclusively to the bathroom narrative as people so often do is to ignore the broader issue and sensationalize something that is really very complex.

What gave you the courage to stand up to the Gloucester County School Board?

The decision to oppose my school board's ruling wasn't much of a decision at all. The question was never "Should I do this?" it was always "How do I do this?" I was facing three years of discrimination if I didn't fight back, and it isn't in my nature to give up on things that violate my humanity. I was just lucky enough to have a supportive household and to have the ACLU on my side. Without these things, I would never have been able to stand up for myself in the way that I have. Of course now, the conversation has moved past me. It is now a nationwide conversation about all trans youth, and knowing that gives me the drive to do my best every day to be a positive representation of the trans community in whatever way, big or small, that I can.

Did you identify as an activist before this fight?

Before this fight I had dreams of living a very quiet life where no one but trusted individuals or partners would know that I was trans. I considered it—and still to some extent do—an irrelevant part of my medical history that no one really had any business knowing, except someone like a girlfriend or healthcare provider. I did not at all consider myself to be an activist. Now, though, with this broader platform that I have, I strive to use it to its fullest extent to raise awareness and advocate where I can, and I imagine that it will always be a part of my life to whatever extent.

What advice would you offer to a young person who decided to take on a similar legal battle to address a violation of rights?

I think my first piece of advice would be that things might take much, much longer than expected. A fight I initially anticipated lasting a year has now stretched on past my graduation, totaling three entire school years of my high-school career. I would also warn them that they may find themselves the public enemy of their town. One might expect cyber harassment or local disdain, but I certainly was surprised at how wrong people were on case details. I had people who hated me with such incredible vitriol that [they] would cite things that were factually incorrect as their basis for such hatred.

Another thing I would say, which is not terribly relevant to me because it does not and never has bothered me, is that there will be plenty of cyber harassment. Perhaps in the form of comment sections, perhaps in direct messages. Either way, it will happen. So, do what you can to prepare and protect yourself for that new reality.

In an ideal world, what would you like the landscape to look like for LGBTQIA youth of the next generation?

Ideally, I would like to live in a world where things like gender and sexuality weren't even something people needed to talk about. It would be nice for someone to be able to introduce themselves as who they are and not face scrutiny or discrimination. Someone's pronouns would be seamlessly and unquestioningly accepted, regardless of their presentation or sex assigned at birth. I do truly believe this future is possible, but it will take a lot of work. Awareness is important, and representation is especially important. It would be nice to see trans people in roles in media that aren't centered on their transness. For example, a buddy cop movie where one character is trans, and it's not an issue, and it's not a major plot twist. That future is coming. However, I also believe the road to that place will be long and hard. The fight is not even close to over.

WE HAVE SOME QUESTIONS
FOR JASON COLLINS

Jason Collins and his twin brother, Jarron, both grew up to be professional basketball players. Jason played thirteen seasons in the NBA, including seven with the New Jersey Nets, three with the Atlanta Hawks, and one with the Boston Celtics. In 2013, he came out, becoming one of the first publicly gay athletes in a major North American sports league to do so. This opened up a much-needed dialogue about LGBTQIA players in the pro sports world. In 2014, *TIME* magazine named Jason one of the "100 Most Influential People" in the world.

Could you talk about yourself as a teenager, and if you recognized your sexuality back then?

I knew I had different feelings, and different crushes in junior high. I had a crush on my history teacher, Mr. Simms. But I kept it all to myself. I thought, "I'm going to date the right girl and it will make [my feelings for boys] go away." But that didn't happen. Then, when I was about sixteen, my dad's brother, Uncle Mark, came out as gay.

Did that give you some comfort?

No, it scared me. I saw how my uncle was treated by some family members, who said homophobic things when he was out of the room. So I didn't come out till my early thirties. I had been engaged to be married [to a woman], but I broke that off in 2009. And then I didn't date anyone. But eventually I came out to some friends and in the winter of 2011 I came out to my aunt. I felt safe with her. She had given me signals, like using gender-neutral pronouns when asking about my love life, that suggested she might know. When I came out to my Uncle Mark, he laughed [and] said "Oh, I knew when you were five years old when we watched a game show with models and bodybuilders, and you only wanted to talk about the men."

So, what your aunt did, is that part of the behavior you would recommend to be a good ally to people who are not yet out but who you think might be gay?

Yes, I would say the more you can wear your heart on your sleeve, the better you are as an ally. There are ways you can show you're supportive. You can post positive things on your social media, comments supporting LGBTQIA rights, supporting equality. You can use gender-neutral pronouns. Or talk about gay friends or people you know who are gay in a normal, positive way. Those are good ways to signal to someone that they are safe with you.

Can you talk some more about when you came out publicly, while you were playing for the NBA?

So in the spring, summer, and fall of 2012, I began coming out to friends and family. And then that winter I came out to my grandmother. That was the hardest, because she was very religious. At the time, I was struggling with some issues in my relationship with my mother. And actually it was because of our problems that my mother, in talking about me, ended up telling my grandmother that I was gay. She was totally great about it. She said, "That's fine that he's gay but what's not fine is your relationship. You two have to fix that!" So she got us to go to therapy together and work things out.

In late February 2013, on the last day of the draft, I was traded from Boston [the Celtics] to DC [the Washington Wizards]. That was a shock. Being traded is like getting a new job. And I decided I wanted to come out then. I just felt like I was sick and tired of living a lie. And I wanted to be able to go on a date! When I moved there were six and a half weeks of ball left to play. So I called my agent and came out to him. He and I talked about whether I should come out right away or wait till after the season ended. We decided I should wait. It was very hard for me to be silent at that time, especially because I was now living in DC while the Supreme Court case*

*On June 26, 2013, the Supreme Court struck down the Defense of Marriage Act, clearing the way for the legalization of same-sex marriage nationwide.

was going on. As an athlete and a gay man, I wanted to be a voice. But my agent convinced me we had to plan, because haters are going to use ammunition to stop you from playing.

I was very lucky because [former NBA player] John Amaechi had come out before me [after he retired]. He was a great mentor. I called him and he said, "You have to prepare yourself mentally to be called the Gay Athlete." Before that I was called the Ultimate Team Player. I was used to labels. It was just one more label.

But I also had to educate myself. I knew about lesbians and I knew about gay men. And I knew more or less about bisexuality. But I didn't know about transgender issues. I had to learn the history and the language. I had to learn about GLAAD and GLSEN. Now I'm on [LGBTQIA rights organization] boards.

Can we talk a little bit more about being an ally, for students and fellow teammates, after someone comes out?

One of the things I would suggest is if you have a friend in school who has just come out, you might find a teacher who can help you connect with GLSEN to make your friends feel safer on campus. There are also some other organizations. The NBA partners with Athlete Ally (athleteally.org) and A Call to Men (acalltomen. org). And there's also the You Can Play Project (youcanplayproject.org). It's important to try to create a locker room environment that is free of sexist and homophobic language.

I'd also say if you come out to your teammates and coach, get your team or school to write down what the culture should be. "Our school, or our team, is going to be a place that . . ." So that when people stray from that, you can go back to the message and say, "Hey, this isn't our culture. This is."

Is it a particular challenge to be both a black man and gay?

Coming out for a black man can be very difficult because of the church. It's very powerful in the black community. Finding a church that binds instead of divides, that spreads "Love is Love," and acceptance, is important. If you are in a church that divides, it's important to confront that church and challenge them.

After I came out, I'd go to parties and still be the only black person. I talked to my Uncle Mark about it and he said, "It's a microcosm of the rest of the world. There is racism in the gay community." You wouldn't think so. You'd think that people who were sensitive about acceptance would be more welcoming. Again, it's up to people to speak up, challenge. I do. Or I leave!

In the end, everything comes from leadership. Right now, our leadership is so anti-LGBTQIA, anti-Muslim, anti-immigrant. It's so disheartening. But you've got to keep fighting! Because we are the majority. The majority are good. I like to believe that every team is stronger when you empower the last person on the bench. When you make them feel they are part of the team. You get them on their feet, and then the whole team is stronger.

Spotlight on
FIERCE

Once upon a time there was a place in New York City where LGBTQIA youth could get together and be themselves: the "Queer Pier." Jutting into the Hudson River at the edge of Greenwich Village, the Christopher Street pier served as a hangout, safe space, and outdoor clubhouse for some of the most vulnerable members of a vulnerable population. Many of them were homeless. Many of them were also people of color. With few or no resources, they relied on a network of social services found on or near the pier, including mobile medical units, food banks, and free social events. But in the 1990s, Greenwich Village started to change. Then Mayor Rudy Giuliani began sanitizing the area with "quality of life" policies. Developers put up shiny high-rises. The Queer Pier was scooped up into the jaws of gentrification. The kids were no longer welcome.

But that didn't stop them from getting . . . fierce.

Founded in 2000, Fabulous Independent Educated Radicals for Community Empowerment, or FIERCE, got their start fighting to keep a toehold at the Christopher Street pier. Since then, the group has expanded into a vital leadership-building organization specifically for LGBTQIA youth of color. The group leads workshops, offers internships, and promotes the strength and competency of their members so that they can go out in the world to fight for themselves and their dignity. FIERCE campaigns have fought police harassment, created safe spaces for LGBTQIA youth, and worked to eliminate hate crimes plaguing the community. Besides their very public work, FIERCE also offers a much-needed sense of community for a group of people who have not always had a place to turn to.

"LGBTQIA youth of color share a lot of the same challenges," explains Mustafa Sullivan, FIERCE's executive director and a member since the group's early days. "They don't necessarily have allies in the mainstream conversation." Nor do they have allies among their own people. LGBTQIA youth of color often exist at the intersection of race, religion, gender, and immigration issues, shunned by families whose traditions do not allow for nonconforming expression, or victimized by cycles of poverty and abuse. The camaraderie FIERCE offers goes a long way toward improving the lives of its members in the future, but also in the day-to-day. In any given week, the FIERCE Facebook page might be announcing a poetry slam, a sex ed workshop, a march on City Hall, or a night of candle making. Reinforced by these gatherings, young people are made ready to take charge of their own lives as well as the world around them.

Since the last election, as Mustafa points out, they're getting a real workout. "A lot more people are out and loud than they were before. Their voices are getting louder." We're hoping FIERCE keeps turning up the volume.

RACIAL JUSTICE

Where does racism come from?

Whoever even came up with the idea that the color of a person's skin, or the ethnic group to which they belong, makes them better or worse than anyone else?

Some evidence suggests that racism first appeared in Europe in the thirteenth or fourteenth centuries. That's when people first made the cockamamie connection between Jewish people and the devil. Religion was an organizing principle in most of the power structures of the Middle Ages, and Europe was ruled by Christians. The anti-Semitic myth that Jews were a "contaminated race" would flourish into the twentieth century, leading eventually to the murder of six million Jewish people during the Holocaust.

Meanwhile, exploration and trade brought Europeans into increasing contact with darker-complexioned people from Africa, Asia, and South America. Often considered heathens (people who don't believe in God), many of these non-Europeans were converted, enslaved, or sometimes both. By the time white settlers made their way to the "New World," prejudice toward anyone who didn't look like a boiled potato in doublet and hose was pretty well established.

The history of racism in America is long, complex, and painful. From the genocide of Native Americans to the enslavement of Africans, from the Chinese Exclusion Act to Japanese American internment camps, from today's anti-Muslim travel ban to tomorrow's border wall, our country has been infected since birth with the scourge of bigotry. And though we've made tremendous strides against the disease through legislation, education, and straight-up activism, we are still a long way from a cure.

Racism continues to express itself in our culture. Some of its manifestations are pretty obvious; others are more subtle. Thankfully we've got help understanding it all from some very interesting and engaged people out on the front lines of the battle. Read on and see what *you* think.

WHAT WE TALK ABOUT WHEN WE TALK ABOUT RACIAL JUSTICE

FOR NATIVE AMERICANS
→ CHALLENGES

CULTURAL ERASURE

The Dawes Act of 1887 was designed to "kill the Indian, save the man"— to assimilate Native people into mainstream white society. The act divided and redistributed tribal lands. Around the same time the boarding school system was established. Children were taken from their homes, given English names and Euro-American clothing and haircuts, forced to attend Christian church, and prohibited from speaking their indigenous languages. They were also commonly subjected to physical and sexual abuse. The explicit goal of these schools was to completely eradicate indigenous cultures. But many Native people today are working hard to reclaim and preserve their culture, engaging in traditional arts and spiritual practices, and recovering and teaching nearly lost languages.

NATIVE LAND DISPOSSESSION

From the moment white Europeans came to this continent, they displaced the indigenous people who were already here. By 1830, several centuries of theft of tribal lands (and lives) became official law: the Indian Removal Act of 1830 pushed Native Americans onto federal territory west of the Mississippi. Decades more of warfare and forced relocation followed, resulting in the reservation system, in which tribes are granted certain limited plots of land. Historically, these were the least desirable areas—isolated and hard to farm. The scarcity, remoteness, unfamiliarity, and resource deficiency of these lands made it very difficult for Native people to develop strong economies of their own or to have strong economic relationships with surrounding non-Native communities.

POVERTY

As of 2016, nearly 27 percent of Native Americans and Alaska Natives live in poverty. There are a number of factors that contribute to this: legal systems imposed by the federal government that hinder economic growth, widespread lack of assets to use as collateral for loans for businesses and development, an absence of financial institutions on tribal lands, staggeringly high unemployment rates (up to 85 percent on some reservations), deficient educational resources, low high-school graduation rights, geographic isolation, and limited internet access.

RESOURCE EXPLOITATION / ENVIRONMENTAL RACISM

Ironically, some of those lands allotted for reservations turned out to have valuable deposits of fossil fuels or mineral-rich ores. For example, between 1944 and 1983, companies mined lands belonging to the Navajo Nation to provide uranium to the federal government, which was using it to build nuclear weapons. As the Cold War and the nuclear arms race died down, the companies abandoned over five hundred mines and left behind tons of nuclear waste, which has been linked to widespread uranium contamination in soil, water, and people's bodies, as well as high rates of cancer and other radiation-related illnesses. The recklessness of the mining companies and government regulators is an example of environmental racism.

SUICIDE RATES

Suicide rates among Native people are at least twice the national average and as much as ten times on some reservations. The number is particularly high among youth. Lack of access to mental health resources combined with high rates of poverty, unemployment, domestic violence, sexual abuse, alcoholism, and drug addiction have created what is being called a crisis.

FOR ALL PEOPLE OF COLOR
→ CHALLENGES

EDUCATION INEQUALITY

Unfortunately, even though the landmark Supreme Court decision Brown v. Board of Education officially ended segregation in public schools in 1954, not everyone gets an equal opportunity for education. Two-thirds of students of color still attend majority-minority public schools, which are often under-funded and disproportionately policed, contributing to the school-to-prison pipeline (more on that on page 90). Complex state funding rules can often mean more tax dollars going to schools in majority-white neighborhoods. School ratings impact real estate values. People send their kids to private school. All of this further contributes to racial and class divides.

EMPLOYMENT DISCRIMINATION

Multiple studies over several decades have shown that the unemployment rate for black college graduates is typically almost twice that of white grad-uates. Sadly, this hiring bias often begins before a job candidate even walks in the door. In 2014, researchers from several universities sent out 9,400 fake résumés for jobs around the country. The result: candidates with so-called typically black names (Deshawn Jefferson, Aaliyah Jackson) were 16 percent less likely to get called in for job interviews than people with so-called typically white names (Cody Baker, Claire Kruger) even though the résumés were the same.

HOUSING INEQUALITY

Racial steering
Racial steering is when real estate brokers either guide people toward certain neighborhoods or fail to give them the full range of housing options based on the buyer or renter's race, either because of unconscious bias or in a conscious effort to keep neighborhoods segregated. The Fair Housing Act was passed in 1968 to protect prospective renters and buyers from this kind of discrimination. But this law is often violated by sellers, landlords, and real estate brokers.

Redlining
This is when services are denied to certain neighborhoods based on their racial makeup, due to the perceived financial risks of investing in such areas. Examples include: denials of loans, credit cards, or insurance; absence of certain kinds of stores and financial institutions; and lack of service by food delivery companies or cabs. Then there's also *reverse redlining*, which is when institutions actually target certain neighborhoods for higher interest loans, on the assumption that residents will default on payments and end up owing the institution much more money.

Gentrification
An influx of wealthier people into a neighborhood alters its culture. Gentrification usually means the displacement of lower-income people of color by white people.

THE PRISON INDUSTRIAL COMPLEX (PIC)

In 1961, in his farewell address, President Dwight D. Eisenhower warned the country of the dangers of the "military-industrial complex." He was talking about the way government and the defense industry were getting together to influence public policy and expand the profitable production and sale of arms. Kind of one hand washing the other. The prison industrial complex, or PIC as it's commonly referred to, is very similar. The PIC is businesses making money by helping the government build and maintain prison systems, and the government offloading their responsibilities to the private businesses.

Throughout the country, black people are incarcerated at five to ten times the rate of white people. Latinx people are incarcerated about twice as much as white people. People who have been incarcerated often face employment discrimination and are denied public housing and assistance. They can end up in a cycle of poverty that may result in breaking laws in order to survive, which often lands formerly in-carcerated people back in jail or prison.

Mass incarceration separates and oppresses people of color.

POLICING

Police brutality

There's really no escaping this in today's society. Sandra Bland. Eric Garner. Michael Brown. Rekia Boyd. Freddie Gray. Tamir Rice. Philando Castile. The list goes on. All black people killed by police. All just in the past ten years. There are also, of course, nonfatal incidents of law enforcement aggression against people of color, like the assault by a white officer of fifteen-year-old Dajerria Becton at a McKinney, Texas, pool party. This sort of violence against people of color has always existed in our country, but now that we have cell phones and social media, it's getting harder and harder to ignore. Which is good—*it shouldn't be ignored.*

Stop and frisk
In New York City, the police department's stop-and-frisk policy—when officers stop a citizen to search for weapons—was long hailed as a method for getting guns off the streets. But the numbers proved something else. According to the ACLU, guns are only found 0.2 percent of the time; 88 percent of the stops between 2002 and 2011 were of innocent people, and 90 percent of those people were black or Latinx. What's more, in the case of Eric Garner, who was accosted by police in Staten Island in 2014 for selling loose cigarettes, the stop-and-frisk policy led to death. Lawsuits, settlements, and court rulings have curtailed what was a widespread stop-and-frisk policy, but it can still be an issue in communities of color.

Prison privatization
Many prisons are privately operated by corporations. Governments pay these corporations based on how many prisoners are in their institutions; that's an incentive to keep a lot of people locked up. Prisons also exploit the cheap labor of inmates, paying them as little as a dollar an hour. Sometimes inmates are working fields that literally used to be parts of slave plantations. The irony is painful.

School-to-prison pipeline
This term refers to a number of trends in school discipline policies that isolate students and put them in early contact with the criminal justice system. Suspensions and expulsions have been steadily on the rise in the past decade, especially for students of color, who are three times as likely to be disciplined as white students. And "zero-tolerance policies" strongly punish students for even mild offenses. Sometimes that punishment includes referring students to law enforcement, especially when there are officers in the school. Students treated this way are twice as likely to drop out of school altogether.

Sentencing laws
According to the ACLU, "sentences imposed on black males are nearly 20 percent longer than those imposed on white males convicted of similar crimes."

Also, there is a much higher percentage of black people serving life sentences without parole than any other race or ethnicity. As the ACLU makes plain, these inequities are a result of unfair treatment of black people at every phase of the criminal justice system, from stop and frisk to trial and sentencing.

REPRESENTATION

In media

Hollywood has a long history of stereotyping African Americans, for example the "mammy," an often-heavyset selfless caretaker of white children, or the "pickaninny," a goofy, gibberish-speaking small black child, or the lazy "Rastaman." And it's the same for other people of color: Asian people are cast as nerds or ninjas, Middle Eastern people as terrorists, Latinx people as housekeepers and drug dealers, Native Americans as mystical medicine people or bloodthirsty warriors.

That is, of course, when they're cast at all! The underrepresentation of minorities in mainstream television and film remains a problem despite high profile social media campaigns like 2016's #OscarsSoWhite.

In sports

The Cleveland Indians, the Atlanta Braves, and the Washington Redskins are a few of the professional sports teams that use caricatures of Native American people in their mascots, logos, and/or team names. Stereotypes like this dehumanize Native American people, which allows for the continuation and spread of bigotry.

APPROPRIATION

Have you ever been to a music festival, or seen pictures of one on Instagram? If so, you've probably seen white festivalgoers wearing "Indian" head-dresses. This is an example of appropriation—taking something from another culture inappropriately, disrespectfully, and without permission. Cultural appropriation is very common in fashion and music videos. It often relies on stereotypes—the Indian headdress, the geisha girl kimono, a sombrero, a bindi, cornrows and box braids—and reduces a culture to externally perceived parts, taking away the voice of the people the culture actually belongs to. People sometimes argue that they are honoring other cultures, but usually there's little or no research done and no consultation with the "honorees"— who *aren't* super honored.

WHITEWASHING

Scarlett Johansson as a Japanese character in *Ghost in the Shell*, Emma Stone as Chinese/Native Hawaiian in *Aloha*, Rooney Mara and Johnny Depp as Native American characters in *Pan* and *The Lone Ranger* respectively—all part of a longstanding Hollywood tradition of *whitewashing*, or using white actors to play people of color. Not only have non-white actors historically been given a very limited range of roles (as we discussed earlier), but sometimes even the roles that *should* be offered to them are given to white people instead!

THREATS TO AFFIRMATIVE ACTION

Affirmative action prohibits discrimination and encourages employers and educational institutions to give special consideration to people who have historically suffered from discrimination, such as women and people of color. President John F. Kennedy and, to an even greater extent, President Lyndon B. Johnson promoted legislation and issued executive orders in the 1960s to support this idea. Fast-forward to today. The current administration is working to roll back affirmative action by suing institutions, using the argument that such policies are racist against white people—despite a 2016 Supreme Court ruling upholding an affirmative action policy.

VOTING RIGHTS

In theory, the Fifteenth Amendment, ratified in 1870, guaranteed non-white people the right to vote. ("People" meant "men": the Fourteenth Amendment had already made that clear.) In reality a lot of states maintained institutional barriers like poll taxes and literacy tests to keep the newly enfranchised voters from exercising that right.

Almost another century passed before President Lyndon B. Johnson signed the Voting Rights Act of 1965, which prohibited these kinds of discriminatory barriers. But . . . that hasn't totally worked out either. Immigrants and people of color are often discouraged from voting by complex voter ID laws and challenges based on unsubstantiated voter fraud questions. Their votes can also be undercut or discounted by gerrymandering, which reorganizes districts to make some people's votes count more than others. Another huge barrier to voting rights is the criminal justice system and felony disenfranchisement, the laws that deny otherwise eligible voters the right to vote if they've been convicted of a felony.

WHITE SUPREMACY

Ever since white Europeans established colonies around the world, the idea of dominance based on skin color has enjoyed alarming support. Slavery was the ultimate expression of white supremacy. It legitimatized a system of dehumanization, bondage, and cruelty that destroyed millions of lives, and inspired a civil war in the United States. Its legacy continues to define much of our national identity.

It's difficult to quantify how many people consider themselves white supremacists. Adherents to the movement do not necessarily identify with the specific term, but rather collect themselves in loose affiliations. They may be neo-Nazis, racist skinheads, Identitarian Christians, neo-Confederates, white nationalists, or members of the Ku Klux Klan. The Southern Poverty Law Center is currently tracking more than 1,600 hate groups, many of them part of the white supremacy movement.

In 2010, white supremacist leader Richard Spencer coined the term "alt-right" as a brand of political conservatism that rejects traditional Republican values. The alt-right promotes white nationalism, or the idea that whites are members of a race that needs to preserve its identity, and primacy. A recent surge of violence in the name of alt-right beliefs—in Charleston, Charlottesville, and Portland—confirms that white supremacy remains a destructive problem in America.

WHITE PRIVILEGE

You've probably heard this term. It refers to the biases in society that favor white people. White privilege is being able to walk down the street without fear of harassment from cops or shop in a store without being the object of suspicion; it's how Scarlett Johansson gets cast in a role for an Asian woman; it's why Justin Bieber can sport baggy pants and a bunch of tattoos and not be called a "thug." White privilege allows white people to distance themselves from other white people who commit terrorist acts, while Muslims are often expected to apologize or explain crimes other Muslims commit. In fact, white people who commit acts of violence in the name of their beliefs are hardly ever called terrorists at all—the list of unearned benefits goes on.

→WHAT WE CAN DO

IN SCHOOL

Fight to change your school mascot. Bring a reasoned argument before the principal. Start a petition. Create an alternative and model the costume.

Combat the school-to-prison pipeline in your school—let your school know that overly stringent and unequal punishment for students of color is not OK. Interview fellow students who have experienced this discrimination and write an article for the school newspaper.

OUT OF SCHOOL

Attend a protest: Check out what Black Lives Matter is up to in your area, contact your local NAACP chapter, join an action to protect sacred lands.

Support legislation: Write your representatives and ask them to support measures that promote equality, like affirmative action. And encourage them to put an end to racist policies like stop and frisk.

AND EVERYWHERE

Listen and learn: The first steps toward eliminating racism are being able to identify it and understanding the places from which it springs. Studying history, listening to our elders, staying open and curious to what's going on around us—these are all ways to participate in change. Remember: knowledge is power.

Be a good ally: Bigotry isn't selective in its victims. It harms us all. If you want to eliminate systems of oppression, being a good ally is a great place to start.

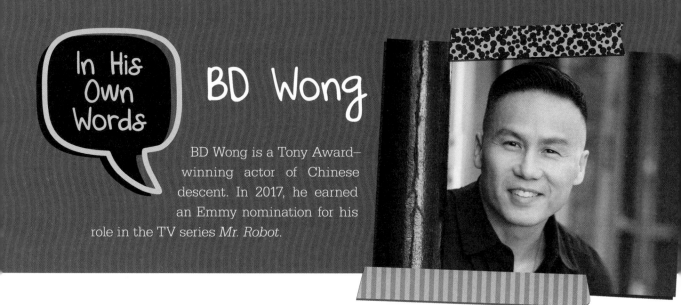

BD Wong

BD Wong is a Tony Award–winning actor of Chinese descent. In 2017, he earned an Emmy nomination for his role in the TV series *Mr. Robot*.

When I was a kid, I wanted to be a storyteller. But as an ethnic minority and an LGBTQIA person, I saw no one on the TV (which back then is where most all the stories were, outside of books) who looked like me. So I felt invisible and ignored and not invited to this big party. The pain I felt motivated me to try to shake things up a little.

I knew what I was getting into when I went into show business. Choosing the issue you want to fight for based on how it touches you or someone you love is a great way to connect to it. That connection will help you remain resilient when battles are lost, and help you stay committed. Public service takes a lot of energy and passion and true caring, so having a personal connection to what you're fighting for will always be your friend.

Go forward with great joy.

WE HAVE SOME QUESTIONS FOR
EVA LEWIS, YOUTH FOR BLACK LIVES

In July of 2016, Eva Lewis and three other girls organized the Chicago Youth Sit-In and March, a silent protest against police brutality in downtown Chicago that drew thousands of protesters. After the march, Eva and her teen friends founded Youth for Black Lives. She is also the founder of the I Project, organized to address the specific, multiple, and often overlapping challenges of young black women.

You organized your first protest with three other young women, all between the ages of sixteen and seventeen. How did you go about it?

My friend Maxine posted on Twitter, and me, Sophia, and Natalie, we all responded to the one tweet in some way, shape, or form. I texted her, "Do you need any help with this sit-in that you're trying to do?" My junior year, there were a lot of protests happening because CPS [Chicago Public Schools] was taking a lot of money out of schools. I would go to meetings of students who were organizing and just take notes and observe. I knew they had press releases, so I brought that information to everybody working on the protests in July, and they were like, "Wait, what? We need a press release?" Then people from BYP100 [Black Youth Project 100] reached out. Because by that time [Maxine's] tweet had gotten a lot of attention and there were thousands of retweets. The BYP100 people were like, "Do you have lawyers?" and we were like, "We need lawyers, what?" So they helped us get a legal team and medics and marshals and all of that. It was just a lot of teamwork and being open to people providing suggestions and communicating.

Do you feel like this demonstration, centering on young women of color, was a radical act in and of itself?

Oh it definitely was. We realized that the only people that responded to Maxine's tweet to help were black girls, and we realized that the only artists that we had performing were black girls, and so we decided to keep it like that. After we saw that trend, we were like, "OK, well, we're at the forefront of movements and this is such a good time to really bring that to the public." And so, we made it clear in our press release, four black teenage girls organized this march.

There were men who were like, "Where are the men?" "You can't do this." "Why are girls doing that?" That happened a lot. But we weren't going to let ourselves be silenced. We were like, "No, this is the work of black girls, period. High-school girls."

What do you think made you four such effective organizers of this protest: was it in spite of or because of your age?

I feel like both. In spite of because we did not know what we were doing. But also we were driven. So, so driven to make it happen. Also, our audacity. I think being young can sometimes be synonymous with being audacious, and our audacity definitely helped us in that we were not afraid. We were like, "We're young, we have time to live, let's go." Like what Youth for Black Lives has done since that protest, talking to superintendents and holding them accountable and listing demands. That was audacious, but in the moment, I don't even feel audacious, I just feel like I'm demanding what I deserve.

WE HAVE SOME QUESTIONS
FOR RASHAD ROBINSON, COLOR OF CHANGE

Rashad Robinson is the executive director of Color of Change, the nation's largest online racial justice organization. Using the power of social media, and the influence of its more than one million members, Color of Change has successfully pushed the online ticketing company Eventbrite to block hate groups, supported amendments to lead poisoning regulations at the Department of Housing and Urban Development, and advocated for improved wages for Walmart workers. OrganizeFor, Color of Change's digital petition and training platform, allows members to access tools to lead change campaigns of their own.

You've been an activist of one kind or another for many years. What inspired you to make a career of social justice work?

I grew up in a small town in eastern Long Island, a community with a very small Black population, though one rooted in a deep and unique part of the African American experience, historically. In that kind of environment, you learn how to organize young because you get agitated by the system from the get-go and then get motivated and quickly learn how to be the agitator—to agitate back. There's a choice, which you either make consciously or unconsciously, or sometimes it gets made for you, whether you are going to become an agitator as a personality trait, or become an agitator as a strategy, as a way of fighting to make things right for the people you see wronged.

I took to the second option.

Color of Change approaches the challenges of racial

justice by leveraging social media in all sorts of
innovative ways. What's the philosophy that guides the
kind of work you do?

Most people, including young people, always start with their voice, and even before that, with their sense of identity in the world, which forms the basis of their voice. Honing that voice is a key entry point to participation, whether it's coming up with your own words or images or actions, or signing on and spreading those of others. The key challenge that links social media to racial justice is not getting lost in our voice alone, thinking that anything will come out of a well-worded post or smart comment or hilarious picture on its own. It's the start, but to get to the end, we have to use social media to drive strategic action—taking the second step, from speaking out to showing up.

Should we feel hopeful that change is happening, or at least in the air?

In these moments, the responsibility is to tap into and channel the new energy in the right ways, whether that's the energy of people feeling their freedom under attack or the energy of people feeling a new kind of hope.

For many Black people in America, and for many oppressed people in America, we didn't wake up the day after the election last year and see something we had never seen before, or face something we had not been dealing with and living with over generations. We are not the people who can say, "This is not the country I grew up in"; for us, it actually is the country, the very same country, in which what happened was not only unsurprising but predictable, given how we've avoided addressing the deep-seated problems of race and of belonging for decades. In the country I grew up in, someone like this can become president, no problem.

The challenge is not to see this situation as new, but how to see yourself in a new way, in your potential and responsibility, as a result of this situation. And that goes as much for the people who are newly woke as those who claim woke status since birth.

WE HAVE SOME QUESTIONS FOR TALIB KWELI

Brooklyn-born Talib Kweli Greene attended New York University and channeled his education into rap and hip-hop. In the late '90s, he and Mos Def formed the group Black Star. Shortly after they got together, New York police shot an unarmed black man named Amadou Diallo forty-one times. In response, Talib and Mos Def gathered forty-one emcees to cut the EP *Hip Hop for Respect*. Since then, Talib has been consistently engaged in art and social activism. In addition to his collaborations with artists like Kanye West, Pharrell Williams, and Dave Chappelle, Talib has also worked with and mentored J. Cole, Kendrick Lamar, and other young rappers.

Were you politically engaged as a teenager, or did you come to it later?

For poor people and people of color there has never been a time that wasn't "politically active." Sure, activism is more mainstream for people who have the luxury of not dealing with oppression, but my family and I were always engaged. Through the '70s and '80s, my mom was a member of NOW, the National Organization for Women. Both my parents were engaged in anti-apartheid work. For conscious black people in the '80s, eliminating apartheid in South Africa was a priority. Also, the consciousness that was prevalent in popular hip-hop of the late '80s aligned with my parents' politics at a time when hip-hop was becoming the most important thing in my life. Being engaged or aware was never something I had to try to do, it was my natural state.

Even though you are famous for "conscious rap," you're

quick to say that artists have no obligation to educate, or represent. What do you say to people who are looking for creative ways to express themselves?

The only responsibility an artist has is to be honest. If I am honest about who I am, I am the son of academics and that is reflected in my music. My responsibility as a member of my community is to show solidarity with all oppressed people and to use my platform to help them. However, I only know this because I was taught. We cannot hold people responsible for things they were never shown or taught. I think artists need political education before trying to engage politically.

You have wisely pointed out that people always want to interview you after police shootings or other tragedies, but we need people to listen before that happens. What are some concrete things we can be doing, daily, to break the racist systems in our communities and in the culture at large?

I follow the lead of the activists doing the work whether the cameras are on them or not, and I use my platform to point to them rather than pretend I have all the answers. I think it's a common mistake to assume that these organizations have not done the work of providing solutions, and it's particularly frustrating when people say it about Black Lives Matter, which like most great activist organizations has done a great job of outlining their solutions on their website. Groups like Advancement Project, Black Youth Project, Campaign Zero, Black Lives Matter, Dream Defenders, and others work very hard to not just identify the problem but to also identify solutions. My answer would be to follow their leads.

You have said in the past that you don't vote. Is that just a personal decision, or is it a philosophy you espouse?

What I have said in the past is not that I never vote, but that voting is not a requirement of an activist or revolutionary. I have been critical of the two-party system, money in politics, and the electoral college for quite some time and I don't give my vote away to politicians who don't work for it. We tell people to vote without making sure they are politically educated or understand the issues. That is a mistake.

Voting in local elections is clearly more effective than [voting in] national ones. Communities voting as blocs is also an effective strategy, one that many black communities have not tried yet. But telling people that their vote counts when it doesn't is dishonest. For example, I live in New York, a Democratic state. When Obama first ran, there was no way he would lose in New York. My vote for him doesn't count. But I voted for him anyway. It was symbolic for me to cast my vote for the first black president. I did not vote for Obama the second time because he was going to win in my state whether I voted or not.

I voted for Hillary [Clinton] as well. I knew she would take New York. So my vote wasn't necessarily a vote for Hillary but it was a symbolic stance against Trump. We cannot guilt young people about voting without being honest about the many mechanisms in our system that are designed to keep power in the hands of straight rich white men.

America is a nation of many immigrants.

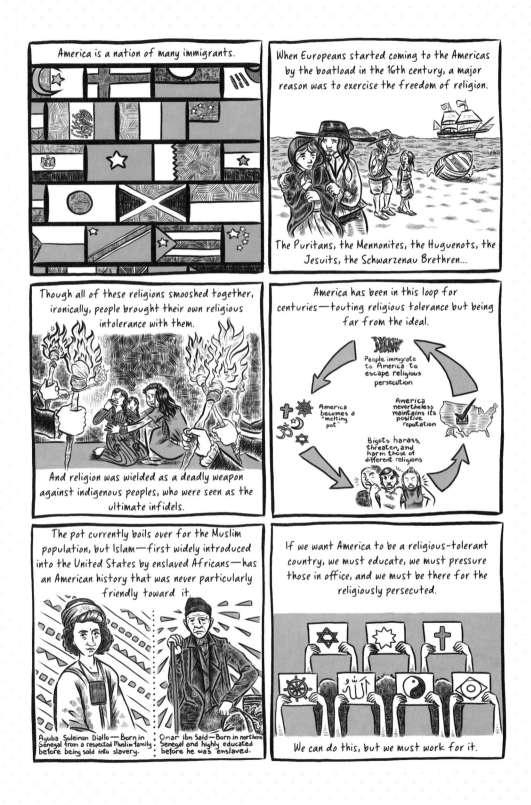

When Europeans started coming to the Americas by the boatload in the 16th century, a major reason was to exercise the freedom of religion.

The Puritans, the Mennonites, the Huguenots, the Jesuits, the Schwarzenau Brethren...

Though all of these religions smooshed together, ironically, people brought their own religious intolerance with them.

And religion was wielded as a deadly weapon against indigenous peoples, who were seen as the ultimate infidels.

America has been in this loop for centuries—touting religious tolerance but being far from the ideal.

People immigrate to America to escape religious persecution

America nevertheless maintains its positive reputation

Bigots harass, threaten, and harm those of different religions

America becomes a "melting pot"

The pot currently boils over for the Muslim population, but Islam—first widely introduced into the United States by enslaved Africans—has an American history that was never particularly friendly toward it.

Ayuba Suleiman Diallo—Born in Senegal from a respected Muslim family before being sold into slavery.

Omar ibn Said—Born in northern Senegal and highly educated before he was enslaved.

If we want America to be a religious-tolerant country, we must educate, we must pressure those in office, and we must be there for the religiously persecuted.

We can do this, but we must work for it.

RELIGIOUS UNDERSTANDING

> "I love you when you bow in your mosque, kneel in your temple, pray in your church. For you and I are sons of one religion, and it is the spirit."
>
> —Kahlil Gibran, writer, poet, and artist

What do you believe in? One God? Two? Thirty-three million? None? Do you wear a yarmulke? A hijab? A cross around your neck? A bindi on your forehead?

Faith is both a personal matter and the main construct of many cultures. What we believe, and how we practice that belief, may bind us to our family, our community, our heritage, and our country. Religious teachings help shape a person's character; traditions give lives context; places of worship provide comfort and a sense of belonging. But no matter what your religious persuasion, if you believe in social justice, you make room for what *other* people believe in.

At first, we called this section "religious tolerance." But Reverend Dr. Katharine Henderson (see page 112) recommended "religious understanding." Tolerance is what you practice when you're stalled on a crowded subway. If you want to build a movement, understanding moves the wheels.

WHAT WE TALK ABOUT WHEN WE TALK ABOUT RELIGIOUS UNDERSTANDING

→ CHALLENGES

ANTI-SEMITISM

Whether you're Jewish or not, you probably know about the World War II Holocaust, during which Nazis murdered more than fifteen million people, including six million Jews. Anti-Semitism, or prejudice against Jewish people, takes many less extreme forms, such as stereotypes and bigoted jokes. That sort of "othering" of people is often what allows bigots to justify violence. In August 2017, a "Unite the Right" rally in Charlottesville, Virginia, drew hundreds of white supremacists, many of whom chanted lines like "Jews will not replace us."

ISLAMOPHOBIA

Travel bans
You may have heard about President Trump's attempt to ban people from seven majority-Muslim countries from entering the United States. Immediately, protesters came together at airports and courthouses to voice their opposition to the discriminatory order and demand its reversal. Thankfully, the people were heard. Organizations like the ACLU went to court and won. But this victory was temporary, and legal battles over the issue continue.

Discrimination against places of worship

There have been efforts around the country to block the building of mosques, usually using zoning laws—the laws that dictate what certain areas of land can be used for. This may be considered a violation of the right to religious freedom, as it denies communities accessible places of worship.

Religious garb discrimination

Religious freedom is guaranteed under the First Amendment of the Constitution. And yet Muslims, particularly Muslim women who wear

traditional coverings, often face discrimination because of their religious garb, and are denied or fired from jobs, suspended from schools, or targeted with harassment.

Surveillance

Since 9/11, Muslim communities have been surveilled by local authorities, FBI, CIA, and the National Security Agency (NSA). Our government has good cause to be vigilant against acts of terrorism from any group. But targeting whole neighborhoods with a "better safe than sorry" approach tends to alienate people and may run afoul of various constitutional rights.

HATE CRIMES

Since the 2016 election, bomb threats against Jewish centers, acts of anti-Semitic vandalism, and violent hate crimes against Jewish people have been on the rise around the country. It's the kind of bigotry that only gets a boost when it comes from the top down. When, for instance, our politicians use language that stokes fear of Muslims, it often gives rise to violence against Muslims—and against Sikhs, people of Middle Eastern descent, or those from the Indian subcontinent. The Council on American-Islamic Relations (CAIR) has reported that Islamophobic hate crimes have gone up a staggering 91 percent since the 2016 election. From ripping off headscarves to attacks on mosques to murder and attempted murder, this is really scary stuff.

→ WHAT WE CAN DO

IN SCHOOL

Start an interfaith club: Interfaith clubs are a fun and meaningful way to get to learn about different religious experiences and traditions. Connect with Interfaith Youth Core (IFYC.org) or the United Religions Initiative (urinorthamerica.org) for the tools and support you'll need to start a club in your school.

OUT OF SCHOOL

Advocate for legislation: In 2015, Senator Richard Durbin of Illinois introduced a bill to deter and punish perpetrators of religious hate crimes, protect refugees who are victims of religious persecution, and make international human rights, including religious freedom, a priority. We can express our support for bills like Senator Durbin's by contacting our representatives.

Support organizations: Explore and/or join up with groups like Interfaith Youth Core, MPower Change (mpowerchange.org), Auburn Seminary (auburnseminary.org), and Jewish Voice for Peace (jewishvoiceforpeace.org).

AND EVERYWHERE

Combat stereotypes: The best way to create religious understanding is by getting to know people who are different from you. Learn about their religions and traditions, read their stories, maybe even organize an event at which people of different faiths share their experiences and perspectives.

WE HAVE SOME QUESTIONS
FOR ZIAD AHMED, REDEFY

Ziad Ahmed is a first-generation Bangladeshi American, who at fourteen years old, founded Redefy (redefy.org) to "boldly defy stereotypes, embrace acceptance, redefine our perspectives positively, and create an active community." He was named one of the "9 Teens Changing the World" by MTV in 2015. In 2016, Ziad was accepted to Stanford University after writing "#BlackLivesMatter" one hundred times as his application essay. He is a student at Yale University.

Redefy is in many ways a platform for storytelling. Can you talk about why this is such an important form of activism?

The crux of the importance of storytelling is that it really is so hard to hate somebody you know, so the hope is that through sharing stories, we can all get to know each other a little better, and subsequently hopefully find more love in between the lines.

What are some of Redefy's most successful initiatives?

I'm really proud of Redefy's #TheGenerationOfNow Conference that we held in 2015 at Princeton University. We brought together twelve incredible speakers to speak on the imperative nature of racial justice to a crowd of over a hundred and fifty. The conversations that stemmed from that event were transformative for many. I'm really proud of the stories that we've been able to share—through our website, social media, events, conversations, assemblies, clubs, and everywhere we possibly can—we believe in passing the mic.

More than any one initiative, though, I'm so proud that there are students who feel more free to be themselves because of our advocacy. Perhaps a team member of ours stood up against the usage of derogatory terms at your school through our Clean Air Campaign, you read a story of someone going through a similar struggle on our website, or you attended one of our events.

Why is it important for young people, though they perhaps can't vote, to get involved in electoral politics?

We might not have a vote, but our future is always on the ballot. We might not have legal legitimacy, but we have the power of the hashtag. In absence of our vote, it's that much more essential that we make our voice heard. If we don't speak up, people assume we have nothing to say or that they can speak for us, neither of which are acceptable. If we care about the world that we will grow up in—the world that the kids we may one day have will grow up in—we have to advocate, engage, and campaign. Our future might literally depend on it.

What would your advice be to other young people who might want to start an organization like yours?

My advice is simple: do it. We all have something that ignites the fire in our stomach, and we should all be running with that. Our age does not limit our activism, and we need to embrace that by taking leaps of faith, and just doing. When we do, we achieve, we thrive, we innovate, we change the world. So, let's do it.

Spotlight on
Eboo Patel and Interfaith Youth Core

In the 1990s, Eboo Patel was a curious college student drawn to social justice and problem solving. So instead of simply volunteering at a homeless shelter, he figured out a way to create a network among shelters, connecting resources to help people find jobs. It was through one of these shelters that he encountered the words of Dorothy Day, founder of the Catholic Worker social movement. He began to learn more about the role that movement played in the lives of people like Martin Luther King Jr., Mahatma Gandhi, Malcolm X, Mother Teresa, Archbishop Desmond Tutu, and the Dalai Lama. Eboo soon took up the idea of being a "social entrepreneur" and set out to make a career out of interfaith leadership.

Since 2002, Eboo's organization, Interfaith Youth Core (IFYC), has been uniting people of differing faiths by focusing on our country's greatest hope: young people. A core IFYC belief is that religious and philosophical traditions should not be a source of division among people but rather a way to make "bridges of cooperation." The group's goal is to inspire "common action for common good." On college campuses all over the country, IFYC convenes Muslims, Christians, Jews, and Sikhs to share their beliefs and ways of living. Together, they explore ideas and challenge assumptions and develop models for in-class programming as well as extracurricular activities.

WE HAVE SOME QUESTIONS FOR REVEREND DR. KATHARINE HENDERSON, AUBURN SEMINARY

Reverend Dr. Katharine Henderson is president of Auburn Seminary, a multifaith organization that teaches leadership, bridges religious divides, and promotes moral courage. She cofounded Face to Face/Faith to Faith, which educates young leaders to be peacemakers around the world.

Can you talk about religious liberty, from a theological perspective?

One of the founding principles of this country is religious freedom. It's just been messed with in a lot of ways recently. The work I do is about bridging the divide. But sometimes it's the intrafaith [within one's own religion] divide that is the most challenging of all. I have more in common with my progressive colleagues who are Jewish, Muslim, Sikh, and Hindu than I do within my own religion. At the People's Climate March [in 2014], we built an Ark that held all religions. A humanist wanted to be on the Ark as well. He hung a sign that said "Atheists on the Ark." Everyone loved that.

What if I don't believe in God? Can people of strong faith make room for that too?

It's a big tent. There's room for a lot of people. We like to refer to people in our [interfaith] community as "people of faith and moral courage." A lot of what it's about is working for justice. That said, faith offers specific traditions and obligations. Caring for the poor and vulnerable; loving thy neighbor as thyself, or as a Sikh friend of mine says, "loving thy neighbor as they wish to be loved," which is harder.

ALEXANDRA STYRON

Some Christians have made choices, like refusing to bake wedding cakes for same-sex marriages. How do we square the principles of a free democracy with the obligation to be nondiscriminatory?

If you serve the public in a business, you must abide by the laws of inclusivity. You don't have to believe in it, but you have to follow the law. Otherwise it's a slippery slope. You're back to [not serving] African Americans at the lunch counter.

How can we bridge the divide so people can stop fearing what—or who—they don't know and see that "other" people are really a lot like them?

It's harder to fix this when people in power are helping to create that divide. Fear is not a principle on which to base one's faith. We're called on to love the stranger. What we try to do [at Auburn Seminary] is to create spaces where people can understand and relate to one another. Like [songwriter] Leonard Cohen says, the cracks are where the light gets in. We try to nurture the cracks.

What do you think are the most productive actions young people of faith can do to participate in the advancement of religious understanding?

Tell your story. Listen to other people's stories. Practice that all the time.

Talk to your family. Gain wisdom from them and share your own wisdom. Storytelling is important in all spaces.

Mine your religious heritage. Or if you have none, find out why.

Develop your own faith.

Break out. Branch out. Figure out what you care about, what breaks your heart, and go to that.

Learn as much as you can and do something! Don't just stay at your computer. March!

Be of service. Find a way out of yourself and do for others.

What does the world you want to live in look like? Cultivate your imagination.

WE HAVE SOME QUESTIONS
FOR BASSEM YOUSSEF

Egyptian-born Bassem Youssef's first career was as a cardiothoracic surgeon. After tending to the wounded in Tahrir Square during the 2011 Egyptian revolution, he decided to do something different. That same year he uploaded his first satirical show about politics on YouTube. It got more than five million views in the first three months. He was soon hosting his own TV show, *Al-Bernameg* (or "The Program"), and kept up a relentless assault on Egypt's political leaders. His humor enlightened and amused millions of viewers—and got him arrested for insulting Islam and then president Mohamed Morsi. Ultimately Bassem and his family were forced into exile; they now live in Los Angeles, California. He's the author of *Revolution for Dummies: Laughing through the Arab Spring* (Read it. It's really funny) and is the subject of the 2016 documentary *Tickling Giants*.

What were you like as a teenager?

I had a regular nerdy life as a teen. I was good at sports as well as academics. I was not politically active, like many young people in Egypt, because after a thirty-year stagnation, you just have resentment toward the status quo.

In response to a totalitarian regime, you did something really courageous: you literally laughed in the government's face. When you were making your TV show *Al-Bernameg*, did you ever think to yourself, "I may be a little bit crazy!"?

I actually was more concerned with presenting a good show. If the tone was softer, it would be doing injustice to the art of satire. We could not ignore what was happening and just do cheap laughs. So I wasn't thinking how brave I was. I was thinking about the next episode.

In 2011, the young people of Egypt started a revolution to fight for justice and to have their voices heard. Are there some lessons you can share from your experiences back home?

It is much more difficult to change people's perceptions than [to] change regimes. Education, justice, and awareness go a long way. It is a much longer process and we can't be impatient with it.

You have said, "Satirists are not activists. They are not freedom fighters. It's up to the people to take the next step." What do you think those steps might be, especially for young people?

If you are talking about western democracies, they should organize, and get out the vote. For our part of the world [the Middle East], well, it is much more complicated, and I think things will get much worse before they get better.

What gives you hope about the world for your children's generation?

They are more exposed to sources of information: internet, open skies, user-generated content. [In the future] it will be very difficult for governments to control information and narratives.

WOMEN'S RIGHTS

> "We hold these truths to be self-evident, that all men are created equal. . . ."
>
> —The Declaration of Independence

Right. But what about women?

Apparently, for the Founding Fathers, the answer was "not so much." For as long as these states have been united, ours has been a country dominated by men. Coverture laws, brought over from England, held fast on these shores for two centuries. These laws kept married women from owning property, from controlling their wages, and, if their husband died, from being given legal guardianship of their children. Women couldn't vote, couldn't petition for divorce. And of course enslaved women had no rights at all.

But then . . . hallelujah . . . along came the feminists! Beginning in the mid-nineteenth century, legions of fierce women started banding together to secure all kinds of rights, some of which we now have the luxury of taking for granted. The first-wave feminists fought hard for suffrage, though it would take more than seventy

years before women finally got the vote. Then, in the 1960s, the second wave notched victories in areas like reproductive rights, marriage equality, and representation in the workforce. And, for the last couple of decades, third-wave feminists have continued smashing the patriarchy through Title IX cases, the outing of sexual harassers, and the introduction of cultural concepts like intersectionality. Women are making extraordinary advances. Plus, as we saw from the many male faces at the 2017 Women's Marches, feminism isn't just for women anymore. But still: *Madam* President? Persistence remains the name of the game.

So, are you ready to start another wave?

WHAT WE TALK ABOUT WHEN WE TALK ABOUT WOMEN'S RIGHTS

→ CHALLENGES

BODY SHAMING

Ever notice that women are disproportionately judged on their appearances? Either praised for their Barbie doll–like features, or criticized for being too skinny, too fat, too short, too tall. Body shaming can be extremely psychologically damaging for young women, and body-positive activists think it's about time it changed.

DOMESTIC VIOLENCE

Domestic violence is violence perpetrated at home; it takes many forms: sexual violence, psychological intimidation, and physical abuse. Around three in ten women and one in ten men have experienced one of these forms of abuse. Part of the problem is that victims of domestic violence often don't feel like they can speak out. This is especially true for people of color and LGBTQIA people, who don't always feel safe calling the police. Ditto for undocumented immigrants, because their citizenship status makes it dangerous to contact any authorities.

SEXUAL HARASSMENT

Unwanted attention of a sexual nature continues to be an impediment for many women in the workplace and elsewhere. Men have often used positions of power to solicit sex, intimidate their victims, and buy silence. The recent #MeToo movement, which resulted in a cascade of women coming forth with their stories and the subsequent firing of their male assailants, speaks to the pervasiveness of the problem.

SEX TRAFFICKING

Sex trafficking is a form of modern slavery in which people are forced to commit commercial sex acts, including making pornography, and prostitution. People of all genders are victims of trafficking, but women and trans people are uniquely vulnerable. Many victims of sex trafficking are children.

SEXUAL VIOLENCE

Sexual violence takes many forms. It can be anything from verbal sexual harassment, to indecent exposure, to rape. The perpetrator and the victim can have any relationship, including being intimate partners. Incest is another form of sexual violence. It can be useful to think of sexual violence as a cultural problem—a symptom of what is sometimes called rape culture, or the normalizing of sexual assault against women.

SLUT SHAMING

Slut shaming is when women are criticized for seeming not to conform to traditional ideas of modesty. This can be based on appearance or perceived behavior: sometimes girls are told they shouldn't wear short skirts or low-cut shirts because it's too "trampy." Or if a girl hooks up with more than one person, then she's called a "ho." What's particularly wack is there's a total double standard: boys are given props for their sexual exploits, and girls are shamed.

This kind of bullying has been linked to depression in young people, and even suicide. It's serious. And seriously not OK.

THREATS TO REPRODUCTIVE FREEDOM

Reproductive rights are all about control over one's own body, specifically the reproductive system. There are many parts to this, including access to information about sexual health and to gynecological exams and procedures, and access to resources such as contraceptives.

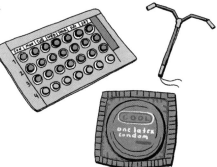

Abortion access is probably the most controversial reproductive right. Efforts to take away a woman's right to choose are threatening all the other reproductive rights as well. Conservatives, especially Evangelical Christians, have been trying to defund Planned Parenthood, the largest and best-known provider of reproductive healthcare in the United States, for a long time. This is because Planned Parenthood provides abortions—which account for 3 percent of their services; 97 percent are super important stuff like OB-GYN care, HIV testing, cancer screenings, prenatal care, and other pregnancy-related services.

In many places that Planned Parenthood serves, people have nowhere else to go for healthcare. Some states, like Texas, have already defunded Planned Parenthood, and the results have been devastating.

THE WAGE GAP

As of 2017, the average woman working full-time makes eighty-two cents for every dollar a man makes. It differs from state to state, but across the board, women tend to make almost 20 percent less than their male counterparts.

And the numbers are significantly worse for women of color. The wage gap also increases with age—older women make even less of a percentage of their male counterparts' wages than they were making earlier in their careers.

→WHAT WE CAN DO

IN SCHOOL

Demand access to sexual health resources: Some cities and states require sexual health education in middle and high school. That includes HIV/AIDS curriculums, condom demonstrations, and accurate information about birth control. Talk with your school administrators and tell them why it's so important to offer this information.

Promote awareness: Every year, the Rape, Abuse, & Incest National Network, or RAINN, organizes a day of action on the third Thursday of September. Host a RAINN Day at your school.

Start programs or clubs: Start a healthy relationship program, with help from End Rape on Campus, or a young feminists club, like the women of the Sacramento Young Feminist Alliance (check out SYFA on Facebook).

OUT OF SCHOOL

Advocate for legislation: Let your representatives know how you feel about the wage gap, sex trafficking laws, child marriage, and safe and legal abortion access.

Put it in words: When you read articles about issues and have something to say, write a letter to the editor.

Support organizations/fundraise: Support Planned Parenthood, Equality Now, Shared Hope, or one of the many other groups that promote women's equality, safety, and health. Then think about ways you can help. Host a fundraiser, have a bake sale, organize a car wash. Donate the proceeds and spread the word!

TALKING WITH CARMEN PEREZ

Carmen Perez is a lifelong social activist and one of the four principal organizers of the Women's March on Washington.

On January 21, 2017, more than half a million people descended on the nation's capital to show opposition to the agenda put forth by our new president, Donald J. Trump. The Women's March on Washington, and the other, affiliated women's marches around the country, became the biggest one-day protest in American history. It signaled the beginning of a new era of activism, and it made the four primary organizers—Bob Bland, Tamika Mallory, Carmen Perez, and Linda Sarsour—famous overnight. But it was hardly their first rodeo. Prior to the march, each woman had distinguished herself in her own field of expertise. And for most of them, social justice has been a lifelong endeavor.

For Carmen Perez, it began on the playground.

"I was always standing up to bullies," she says of her childhood years in Oxnard, California. Growing up in a family of devout Catholics, Carmen was often left at home with her siblings while her mother traveled the world to pray for people. Carmen loved her mom's work ethic and "willingness to give." And though she considers herself more spiritual than religious, it is clear the atmosphere Carmen grew up in made a deep impact. "I used to tell my big sister I was going to change the world," she recalls with a laugh, "though I don't know where I got that kind of swagger."

At seventeen, Carmen went away to college at UC Santa Cruz. While she was there, two events occurred that would determine much of what came after for her. Her sister, then nineteen, died. A short while later, one of Carmen's brothers was incarcerated. Being exposed to the prison system at the same time she was in mourning helped to open her eyes as well as her heart. By the time she graduated, Carmen knew that a life of service, one involving young people, would be her path.

In the years following, she worked for reform in the California prison system, founded Reforming Education, Advocating for Leadership (REAL), and cofounded the Girls Task Force to improve the lives of girls in marginalized communities. Carmen's grassroots work led her to develop a new model for finding solutions to persistent societal challenges. She convened a Youth Summit where kids could caucus on issues like gangs, violence, and malpractice within the penal system. Ideas generated at the meeting were often taken up by the state's policy makers and led to many positive reforms.

In 2005, civil rights legend Harry Belafonte founded the Gathering for Justice to address the racial disparities of mass incarceration; he asked Carmen to join him. Since 2010, she has been the executive director of the Gathering, advocating for prison reform and an end to child incarceration.

When the Women's March was gathering steam and looking for leaders, Carmen was an obvious choice. Since that historic day in January, her full plate has overflowed. She's in near constant demand to speak and to lead. In the end, that's what Carmen tells her niece and nephews forms the basis for engagement and for life. "I always ask them, 'What do you dream of? What will make you happy?'" Clearly, helping to make a better world is Carmen's happy place.

WE HAVE SOME QUESTIONS FOR YASMEEN HASSAN, EQUALITY NOW

Yasmeen Hassan is a lawyer and the global executive director of Equality Now, an international organization focused on achieving a more just world for women and girls through addressing harmful practices like sex trafficking, child marriages, legal inequality, and sexual violence.

Can you tell us what's the most difficult part of your job? Do you ever feel like, "This is too upsetting, I can't do this anymore"?

How can we turn away from girls who need our help because it is upsetting for us? We have to find ways to use what might have upset us to the point of "shutdown" to instead motivate us to work. I don't think I've ever felt that this is too difficult.

So many women and girls, right now, are struggling with the world's worst violence and injustice because of their gender. However, when it happens to young girls, it destroys the future potential of those girls, which we can't let happen. Although change is hard and it takes years and the fight can sometimes feel overwhelming, it is not possible to turn our backs.

What's the most rewarding aspect of your work?

The most rewarding aspect of my work is meeting the amazingly brave and resilient young women and girls who have taken their own personal tragedies and used them to drive change that impacts thousands like them. It is an honor to be able to work with girls around the world who are transforming the societies they live in, and of course, when successful, always heartening to see the change that we help bring about.

Mariam was fifteen when she brought an unprecedented case of incest to court in Pakistan. She won, which helped change the rape laws.

Mary was thirteen when she was raped by her schoolteacher. She had the courage to take on the entire Zambian government, who failed to take action against her teacher. She won, establishing government responsibility for rape in schools.

Wafa was only eleven when she was married to an adult man. She fought to get a divorce from her husband in Yemen, where we are still fighting to outlaw child marriage.

What sort of issues do you focus on in the United States?

The 2016 Gender Inequality Index ranks the United States 43 out of 188 countries, so the United States is not a leader in gender equality! We are focusing on sex trafficking and sex tourism in the United States. Not only do 25 percent of global sex tourists come from the United States, it is a top destination country for sex trafficking. The US average age of entry of a girl into the sex trade is about thirteen to fourteen, which should indicate that these are not women making adult choices, these are girls forced against their will. We work to ensure that abusers are arrested, and that groups promoting sex trafficking (like Backpage and sex tourism companies) are shut down. Further, we need to help victims of sex trafficking and sex tourism be properly identified and protected by the law.

How can young people be helpful activists and good allies in the fight for gender equality here and abroad?

Never forget that no voice is too small to make a difference. Young people today have an activist spirit. If they understand feminism, they will understand how we are all affected when women and girls are not treated equally next to men and boys.

TALKING WITH SOFIE KARASEK, END RAPE ON CAMPUS

Sofie Karasek always wanted to be an activist.

Growing up in Cambridge, Massachusetts, Sofie was super interested in the issue of climate change. She enrolled in her "dream school," UC Berkeley, because of its top-rated environmental science program and history of political engagement.

The dream turned dark pretty quickly. In the fall of 2012, her freshman year, Sofie took a trip with the Cal Berkeley Democrats. While she was sleeping, she was sexually assaulted by a fellow student. Afterward, she spoke up about the attack and discovered that three other women had had similar experiences with the same man. Together, they reported the incidents to the administration. "They said they would look into it," Sofie recalls of their meeting with university officials.

For eight months, the women heard nothing. In the end, the university took care of the matter, resolving the case behind the women's backs. The assailant was allowed to graduate ahead of time with no real punishment, and then he went on to law school. Sofie and her fellow survivors decided to take action.

Bringing their case before the student senate, the women registered a vote of No Confidence regarding the administration. Sofie then went on to file a federal complaint, under the Title IX law. Though the case was dismissed in 2016, because it did not meet the standard of "deliberate indifference," the judge's ruling was largely sympathetic to Sofie and the other plaintiffs, and included harsh words for the university's deliberation process.

During her fight with the university, Sofie's research led her to students with similar complaints at other universities, and they began to organize.

Sofie had become an activist, just not the sort that she had planned.

She cofounded, and served as the director of education of, End Rape on Campus (EROC), one of the country's leading organizations working to stop sexual violence against students. EROC's multiplatform approach to the issue includes direct support for survivors wishing to file complaints, education at all school levels, policy reform work, and advocacy. Since their founding in 2013, EROC has directly assisted more than 180 complainants in Title IX sexual assault cases, spoken to hundreds of students across the country, and spearheaded the implementation of mandatory healthy relationship programs in several states. Sofie has moved on from the organization she helped start, but she always encourages survivors to speak out. "Our stories are powerful," she says. And sadly, there are a lot of stories to be told. Numerous reports in recent years have shown that roughly 20 percent of women are sexually assaulted while in college. LGBTQIA people are also frequent victims of sexual assault on campus, as are cisgender men.

So what else can be done, particularly at the high-school level?

Help change the culture, for one thing. "Look for what's happening at your school that's not OK," advises Sofie. "Are girls being sent home because their clothes are too risqué and 'boys can't concentrate'? Is there slut shaming going on? You can bring that out in the open and push for change." Also, use your local resources as well as advocacy organizations online. EROC, for instance, offers help to students who want to start healthy relationship programs in their high schools. And above all, if you are a victim of assault, don't keep it to yourself. There's lots of support out there. As Sofie now knows, "people want to hear from you."

WE HAVE SOME QUESTIONS
FOR LENA DUNHAM

You probably know writer, director, producer, actress, and author Lena Dunham from her wildly popular HBO show *Girls*—or from the massive backlash and criticism she's gotten as an outspoken woman in the public eye.

You've received a lot of backlash for appearing nude on *Girls*. Was there a moment when you realized you could use your body as a political tool?

I grew up in the art world, where the body was a tool like film or clay. It seemed natural to me that—since I couldn't draw or sing—art utilizing my physical form would be my medium. I was ignorant of just how much rage existed outside these small liberal enclaves about the female form. But the minute I understood, I became more, not less, determined. I knew that the anger I was getting was just a reflection of the anger women experience within their relationships, school environments, etc., for daring not to fulfill an ideal, for being too sexual or not sexual enough. I hope my work and my freedom around these issues is some small contribution to chipping away at the iceberg of judgment and pain surrounding women (cis and trans) and their physicality.

Can you talk about how healthcare and women's rights intersect?

It wasn't until I got sick, really sick, that I understood two things: our healthcare system is classist and our healthcare system is misogynistic. As a white woman with plenty of disposable income, I got what I needed in terms of attention, but I

ALEXANDRA STYRON

was often treated as if my endometriosis [a painful disease of the uterus] was not a serious illness or, worse yet, a symptom of my anxiety disorder (since my medical history reveals clearly I've been diagnosed with an anxiety disorder since the age of twelve). The feeling of going for urgent care and seeing the slight condescension in your doctor's eyes is profoundly painful, as is the eye rolling certain male colleagues can have about stopping work for what they see as, essentially, menstruation. That's why I really never shut up about my mental and physical health. I want every woman to be comfortable being her own advocate without shame, to treat her broken uterus with the same respect she'd treat a broken leg, and to understand mental health challenges do not nullify your physical suffering. Decreasing stigma is my first goal. Increasing access to care is its own, even bigger issue and I hope we will all begin to focus on it in a concentrated and coordinated way.

What do you hope the third wave of feminism will accomplish?

I'm so proud of the young women who are coming on the scene right now. When I was in my teens and twenties, there was a lot of apathy, a lack of awareness of how hard our mothers and grandmothers worked for us. The teens of today are informed, they're obsessed, and they're not stopping until they see change. It humbles me, and I believe that with their knowledge, their access to information, and their ability to amplify their message, maybe, just maybe, I'll get to be a little lazy in my old woman–hood about certain well-trodden issues.

NOW LET'S TALK ABOUT
INTERSECTIONALITY

> "There is no such thing as a single-issue struggle because we do not live single-issue lives."
>
> —Audre Lorde, black lesbian writer, poet, and activist

Dr. Kimberlé Crenshaw, a civil rights activist and scholar, coined the term *intersectionality* in 1989 in an essay on race and feminism. She was following the work of such trailblazers as the Combahee River Collective, Audre Lorde, bell hooks, Cherríe Moraga, and Gloria Anzaldúa, all of whom, as women of color, had taken issue with what they experienced as the privilege of upper- and middle-class white women in the first and second waves of feminism. They felt that the feminist movement was ignoring the *multiple* forms of oppression many women experienced, such as sexism *and* racism, or sexism *and* homophobia, or sexism *and* ableism—or all of the above. For example: a poor, lesbian, transgender, undocumented, disabled Latinx woman? She lives at the intersection of *a lot* of different kinds of oppression. If the feminist movement was going to truly fight for the rights and equality of *all* women, it needed to explore the intersectionality of racism, classism, homophobia, transphobia, ableism, or xenophobia that make many women's experience of sexism so much more complicated. White, straight, able-bodied women need to be effective *allies* in those struggles.

There are many issues that historically haven't been looked at as feminist issues, but taking an intersectional viewpoint can help us see how they are.

For instance, in 2014, the city of Flint, Michigan, in an effort to save money, disconnected from the Detroit water system and started drawing its water from the toxic Flint River, poisoning its predominantly poor and black citizens with lead. In Flint (and the rest of the world), single mothers, women of color, and elderly women disproportionately make up those living below the poverty line. Around ten thousand children in Flint have been exposed to lead and its irreversible health and behavioral effects, which, since women are largely the primary caregivers of children, directly affects the women of Flint. Lead exposure is also linked to miscarriage and other crises for pregnant women, making the situation in Flint a reproductive justice issue as well. So, here we have an intersection of race, class, and gender in what is in part an environmental crisis—a case of environmental racism that is in fact a feminist issue.

An intersectional viewpoint allows us to see how systems of oppression are linked and teaches us that to fight any of them, we must fight all of them. It asks us to think a level deeper about social justice and to consider the unique challenges some groups face. Acknowledging intersectionality requires a little more of our brains, and maybe a little more of our hearts.

WE HAVE SOME QUESTIONS FOR ALICE WONG, DISABILITY VISIBILITY PROJECT

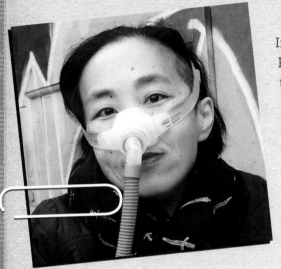

In 2014, Alice Wong founded the Disability Visibility Project in partnership with StoryCorps to amplify the voices of disabled people and their culture. She was a member of the National Council on Disability from 2013 to 2015 and also serves on the advisory board of Asian and Pacific Islanders with Disabilities of California.

Can you tell us a little bit about yourself?

I'm forty-three, born and raised in Indianapolis, Indiana. Currently, I live in San Francisco and have a background in sociology. I went to grad school for medical sociology and worked at the University of California, San Francisco, for over fifteen years. I decided a few months ago it was time for a change and am now an activist full-time while working on the side as a research consultant.

I was born with a neuromuscular disability called spinal muscular atrophy. It means that my muscles get progressively weaker all the time. I used to be able to walk when I was a kid, started using a wheelchair when I was about seven, and then graduated to other supports that allow me to do what I want to do.

Can you talk about your teenage years?

This is funny because I recently got a message on Facebook about my high school's twenty-fifth reunion. I laugh because it's scary that I'm so old now. I also laugh because I hated my high school years. I went to a regular public high school in suburban Indianapolis in the 1990s. It was very white, affluent, and conservative. As a Chinese American disabled teenager who used a wheelchair, I stuck out a lot. I was one of

ALEXANDRA STYRON

those students involved in tons of activities but still felt excluded and lonely. Plus, I experienced outright discrimination from one of my teachers that made me seriously angry at social attitudes. The school was semi-accessible but this was right around the time of the Americans with Disabilities Act (ADA) so "accommodations" wasn't even a term I used when fighting for access. I guess my message to teachers and fellow classmates is: "So many of you were entitled, racist, narrow-minded assholes. I'm sad that you had such low expectations of disabled people like me." If I sound bitter it's because I'm kinda sorta am. That's OK by me because it drove me to find the life I want.

According to the Center for Disease Control, 53 million adults in the US live with a disability. That's not even counting people under eighteen! And yet it doesn't seem like disability rights is high on most people's radar. Do you think that needs to change? And if so, how?

I definitely think that needs to change! For a long time people didn't know much about women's history, the history of LGBTQIA people, Native Peoples, Asian Americans, African Americans, and Latinx people. All of these communities have a history of not having power, resources, or equal rights. Things are getting better for all groups and I feel that there's still a long way to go for people to know that disabled people played a big part in our history as a country. Also, there have been disabled people in every community and too often their disability identity is erased, which is a real shame.

The Disability Visibility Project uses storytelling to expose people with various disabilities to the larger public and to advance conversation on the issues surrounding disability rights. Why and how is storytelling useful as a tool for activism?

Simple answer: we know ourselves best. We each have a unique story that is ours alone. Activism can begin by sharing your life experiences with others and opening people's minds. Lots of people think of activism as rallies and protests but it can start out with a conversation between two people. I love the phrase, "The personal is political." I believe this deeply.

Some people reject the word disability in favor of other phrases, like differently abled, or special needs. How do you think language and labels serve to empower, or disempower?

Everyone goes through their own process on the language they use and how they want to identify. For those who use "special needs" or other euphemisms, I'm not going to shame them. I will be vocal about how I personally reject those terms when describing myself. What I don't like is when people tell me what words I can use. For example, there are some disabled people like me who call ourselves "crip" and are proud of this term. There are many disabled people who find this offensive. I use it to subvert the meaning when historically "cripple" was used to denigrate and stigmatize disabled people. Taking pride is a constant evolving process, and language is one way we show the cultures that we are proud of.

The Americans with Disabilities Act of 1990 (ADA) was the first major US law enacted to protect the civil rights of people living with disabilities. What did it accomplish? What do you think still needs to be done?

A lot of work that remains. The ADA is a major civil rights bill that's ours, it's something we can point to and say, "Hey, this protects our rights as a group." Right now, there are forces out to undermine the ADA. It was never a perfect bill, but weakening it will only make it worse for people with disabilities. The ADA Education and Reform Act of 2017 (HR 620) will make it harder for people with disabilities to fight for access by putting the burden on them to notify and educate businesses.

In 2010, President Obama took a giant step toward providing universal health care for all citizens with the Affordable Care Act. Did the ACA improve healthcare options for people with disabilities? What is at stake now as the ACA is under threat of being dismantled?

The ACA helped people with disabilities in a number of ways. First: people with pre-existing conditions could no longer be denied coverage by insurance companies.

The second thing is that it allows young adults to stay on under their parent's [health insurance] plan a bit longer which can help give time for young disabled adults to transition and afford their own coverage. There's a lot at stake right now. The new (as of this writing) proposed federal budget proposes deep cuts into Medicaid. Medicaid helps many people, not just disabled people. Children, older adults, pregnant women, all of us will be impacted by cuts that will force states to decrease enrollment and services. Medicaid also covers mental health services for more than seventy million poor and disabled people. What's more, if the GOP succeeds in rescinding Obamacare, millions of people would be in danger of losing their insurance and older people will likely pay much higher premiums. I wrote about my Medicaid story in *The New York Times* (5/3/17) to give a sense of what's at stake.

A lot of your work addresses the intersection of disability and other human rights issues: poverty, racism, gender equality. How do you present these ideas together? Do you prioritize or try to look at them as all of a piece?

It's hard to separate these issues, they're all interrelated. Whenever you're talking about one thing, it's critical to look at the issue through multiple lenses, think about how different communities experience them, and to acknowledge the power differential that exists.

What do you think the future of activism on disability rights should be about?

I'd like to see activists from other movements and communities show solidarity with us in meaningful ways. I'd like to see disabled activists in all movements, not just disability rights. I'd like to see new and innovative ways to make activism accessible to as many people as possible. I'd also like to see more media coverage about activism by disabled people. I'd also like to see disabled people working in all the major news organizations.

THE HOW

· · · · · · · · · · · · · ·

Whew. OK. Now you have a lot of information. What are you going to do with it? You're going to kick some activist butt, of course. But how? By reading The How. In the upcoming pages, you'll discover lots of ways to put your passion into action. Whether you're sitting at a computer or walking down the street, spending time with your family or hanging with friends after school, starting your own small business or stopping a big corporation, if you've got an hour or a year, we've got an action for you.

HOW TO BE AN ALLY

A lot of people become social activists because they are sick and tired of being oppressed, of seeing their people marginalized, kicked around, or roundly ignored. But a whole lot of people join the fight and become allies because they cannot turn a blind eye to injustice done to others. They feel, as Emma Lazarus put it, that "until we are all free, we are none of us free." Now's a good time to examine your situation. Do you feel pretty lucky? Are you in a position not only to fight for your own rights but to help other less privileged people get what they deserve? Is so, then consider yourself an ally. But know that being an effective one takes a lot of listening, learning, and some real work.

HERE ARE A FEW STEPS TO GET YOU STARTED

ARE YOU COMING FROM A POSITION OF PRIVILEGE? IF SO, ACKNOWLEDGE IT: This is the big first step. Recognize the ways in which you benefit from systems of oppression. Recognize the ways that other people struggle but you don't. Recognize the ways in which you are safer than others, and therefore the ways that you can safely stand up for what you believe in.

TAKE ACTION: The thing is, we can't just decide to call ourselves allies. Being an ally requires concrete action: showing up and doing the work that is asked of us by marginalized people. (That said, it's important to make sure not to take up too much space—more on that later.)

NEVER LET UP: Allyship is also not a label we get to take off when it's convenient. If you see an instance of racism, sexism, homophobia, transphobia, Islamophobia, or other bigotry, don't stay quiet. This is a 24/7 thing.

LISTEN AND LEARN: Seek out people who are marginalized and ask them to talk with you. Be ready to learn—and to maybe learn some uncomfortable truths. Read books and blogs, listen to podcasts in which people talk about struggles you don't know much about. Listen to your peers who might have more direct experiences. For some of us, this will also mean taking a step back and talking less ourselves.

BUT DON'T EXPECT OTHERS TO EDUCATE YOU: Part of privilege is expecting things to come to us, expecting others to do things for us. A lot of us have been conditioned that way. To be a good ally, we can't put the burden of our own education on other people. People experiencing various forms of oppression have enough going on without having to worry about our education. It's everyone's responsibility to educate themselves; again, listening well to the voices of marginalized people is an important part of this.

BE OPEN TO CRITICISM: No one's perfect, we all mess up sometimes. It's really important to be able to acknowledge mistakes, shortcomings, and blind spots. We've all got blind spots, especially those of us who've grown up with relative privilege and haven't had to think about certain things. Be ready to acknowledge these and to learn from the feedback you get. You might feel defensive at times—take a breath and a step back. Maybe you did mess up; maybe you can learn from it and do better moving forward.

DON'T EXPECT A REWARD: Being an ally isn't about earning points and looking good. It's not always fun, and your work won't always be acknowledged. That's OK. Justice is the real reward that we're all working toward together.

LET'S TAKE SOME EXAMPLES

If you're cisgender, imagine one of your classmates is transitioning. You've overheard other kids in your class saying mean things about this person. Maybe they're refusing to use your classmate's correct pronouns or maybe they're even threatening them. Being a bystander in this situation means being part of the problem, and there are a couple of ways you can manage the situation:

DIRECTLY INTERVENE: Take the jerks aside (or, hey, make a scene!) and let them know how you feel about what they've been saying or doing. If you think that their behavior comes from genuine ignorance, offer to help educate them.

TELL A TEACHER OR OTHER SCHOOL OFFICIAL: Yeah, we know, not cool, but especially if someone is threatening violence, sometimes this is the best move. And in that situation, being cool is no longer the most important thing.

REACH OUT TO THE PERSON BEING BULLIED: Let them know that you stand with them. Ask what they need and how you can help.

HERE ARE A FEW OTHERS: If you're white, imagine you hear another white classmate using a racial slur. Or if you're a boy, imagine another boy in your class is sexually harassing one of your female classmates. The same steps as above apply.

KNOW YOUR RIGHTS!

Thanks to the US Constitution, you have certain inalienable rights. Even if you aren't a citizen, you are protected by our country's foundational charter and its twenty-seven subsequent amendments. (Need more specifics on those rights? Check out whitehouse.gov/1600/constitution.)

Our great and mighty Constitution details not only what we may do but what our government *may not do TO us*. It is the backbone of our democracy, and most of the time, it works like a charm.

Except when it doesn't.

The fact is it's an imperfect world and we are an imperfect country. Things don't always go the way they should. Every day, people's constitutional rights are violated.

Sometimes it's obvious, and happens in a flash: you are stopped and frisked by police without proper cause, your sister suspects she was turned down for a job because she wears a hijab. But often, rights violations are more subtle and systemic, like gerrymandering. Or the practices of our national prison system, which incarcerates African American men at a disproportionately high rate.

Recently we've seen a worrisome trend in Washington at the highest levels. The attempted ban on travel from majority-Muslim countries, threats to sue the press for libel, a promotion of the idea that athletes should be jailed for kneeling during the national anthem. These are all threats to our constitutional rights. And they are coming from within our government.

It's never been a more important time to KNOW YOUR RIGHTS!

And thankfully, to help with that, we have the American Civil Liberties Union (ACLU).

Founded in 1920 to protect antiwar speech, the ACLU is now the country's preeminent organization working, according to their mandate, "to defend and preserve the individual rights and liberties guaranteed to every person in this country by the Constitution and laws of the United States." The ACLU helped to defend John Scopes when he tried to teach the theory of evolution in 1925; it joined the NAACP's fight to desegregate schools in the Brown v. Board of Education case of 1954; it even defended the right of a Nazi group to march in Skokie, Illinois, in 1978, because, hey, rights are rights and they must be defended for everyone or they don't work for anyone.

These days the ACLU represents immigrants, LGBTQIA students, pregnant women, disabled children, victims of torture, Muslims and Christians and Jews—really anyone whose fundamental liberties are being infringed upon. The organization protects free speech, works for criminal justice reform, educates, and advocates. It defends the very best of our American ideals and helps us to understand exactly what those ideals are. Want to know more or get involved?

Go to ACLU.org (and be sure to check out "People Power," a grassroots mobilization project that is engaging volunteers to join the new resistance movement).

Spotlight on
NYCLU Teen Activist Project

On Mondays in a skyscraper at the southern tip of Manhattan, you can find twenty high-school kids, a mix of genders, ethnicities, and sexual orientations, sitting down after school for an intensive discussion about civil liberties, often with legal experts, constitutional scholars, or community organizers. This is the New York Civil Liberties Union Teen Activist Project (TAP).

Established more than twenty years ago, TAP is a selective project offering paid internships to motivated students interested in social justice. Over the course of the school year, participants explore topics like reproductive rights, immigration, policing, LGBTQIA issues, and students' rights. They're coached on how to speak before large groups, trained to attend marches, and encouraged to consider leadership opportunities within their own communities. One day they're on Broadway handing out rights-focused pamphlets. The next day they're testifying before the city council on the need for sex education funding.

"My mother always says, 'If you're bothered by something, don't just talk about it. Do something,'" explains Ben, a TAP member and student at Beacon High School in Manhattan. For Angelica, who lives in the more conservative borough of Staten Island, it's about being able to take what she's learned and share it with people back home. Marlon, an outspoken student at the Lab School in Manhattan, wants to be a lawyer, and balances TAP work with participation in Model UN, as well as their school's Gender and Sexuality Alliance and HIV/AIDS Action Club. Not surprisingly, many of the TAP students are interested in the law and all of them are bound together by a passion for justice. From here it's off to college, and the world beyond—a world made better because of kids like them.

Want to "tap" your local ACLU chapter to start a program like this? Go to ACLU.org to inquire and learn more.

ROCK THE VOTE: ALL ABOUT VOTING

One of the great slogans of the American colonial era was "no taxation without representation." The colonists felt that because they didn't have an elected representative in the British Parliament that governed them, the laws and taxes being imposed on them were unjust. Their outrage started as editorials, boycotts, and protests, which led to the Revolutionary War, the Declaration of Independence, and the founding of our country. Throughout our country's history, voting rights have been a battleground. Our Constitution did not originally say explicitly who could vote. Many people were excluded, especially people of color and women. Through strong organizing and enormous sacrifice, that changed.

Each expansion of the right to vote brings us closer to true democracy, but every challenge again widens the gap. In some states and some elections, voter rights are still impeded. Voter ID laws have been implemented and voting districts subjected to gerrymandering in order to give one party a political advantage.

Voting is the cornerstone of our democracy. Even if you're too young to vote, it's important to understand the process and know how this crucial right is—and sometimes *isn't*—protected. People literally died for a right that many of us now take for granted—and too many Americans don't even bother to exercise!

→THREATS TO VOTING RIGHTS

VOTER ID LAWS

In theory, Voter ID laws are meant to ensure that all people who have a right to vote can, and that those who are ineligible do not. But in practice, Voter ID laws are often unfairly applied, and used for political purposes. Laws that require specific forms of identification at the polls are particularly terrible. Here are some reasons why:

At least twenty-one million Americans don't have a government-issued ID; they are disproportionately people of color.

Getting an ID can be expensive—it requires travel and paying fees, things a lot of people can't afford.

Voter ID laws actually cost a lot of money to put in place—taxpayer dollars. Like, millions and millions of dollars.

The forms of ID that are allowed in states are pretty discriminatory. In Texas, for instance, voters can use concealed weapons permits, but not student IDs.

Studies show that voters of color are much more likely to be asked for ID.

Some politicians say we need these laws because our system is overrun by voter fraud. But that's the real fraud—a Loyola Law School study published in *The Washington Post* shows that between 2000 and 2014, only thirty-one credible instances of voter fraud occurred *out of one billion votes cast.*

GERRYMANDERING

The first gerrymander was in 1812, when Elbridge Gerry was governor of Massachusetts. The Democratic-Republicans' effort to divide the Federalist vote resulted in a map that looked, to artist Gilbert Stuart, like a giant salamander. After Stuart highlighted the shape, newspaper editor Benjamin Russell renamed it a "Gerrymander."

OK, so this is kind of complicated, but bear with us:

Everyone lives in an *electoral district*. You are a *constituent* of that district and can only vote from within that district. *Gerrymandering* is the process of remapping these districts in order to benefit a certain political party or group. Drawing the boundaries of an electoral district in a certain way controls the number or makeup of the constituents in that district.

There are basically two kinds of gerrymandering:

Cracking is when certain types of voters are distributed throughout different districts so that they can't develop a strong voting bloc to support a particular candidate or policy. A good example would be breaking up an urban area with a majority population that tends to vote progressive and recombining those smaller pieces with different suburban districts whose majority populations vote conservative.

Packing is when certain types of voters are concentrated into one electoral district so that their influence is reduced overall. For example, a number of progressive-majority neighborhoods are all packed together in one single district so that the majorities in all the remaining districts are conservative.

Gerrymandering is often based on race and used as a tool to suppress the votes of people of color. The result is some people get representation and tax dollars and access to all the nice things that tax dollars buy, and other communities get thrown aside and don't have much say. Pretty unfair, right?

TURNING EIGHTEEN ON OR BEFORE THE NEXT ELECTION? HERE ARE SOME TIPS TO GET YOU STARTED:

REGISTER: Go to vote.gov to see what the voter registration rules are in your state and how to get an absentee ballot if you're going to be away on Election Day.

VOTING RULES: To find out your state's voting rules, go to usa.gov/election-office and learn how and when you can vote.

At your polling place, there are a few things everyone will probably need—though each state has different requirements (some are stricter than others):

A driver's license or state ID card number

The last four digits of your social security number

A local address or ZIP Code

If you get to your polling place and your right to vote is challenged, here are some important things to know:

In many states, you have the right to give a sworn statement to your poll worker that you are qualified to vote and cast a regular ballot.

If your poll worker insists that you are not on the list of registered voters, first ask them to double-check. If you're not there, ask that they look at the supplemental list of voters that often contains voters who registered close to Election Day. If there's no supplemental list or you're not on it, ask that they look at the statewide system to see if you need to be on a different polling list. And finally, if they still can't find your name, ask for a provisional ballot. Your qualifications will be investigated by election officials after Election Day.

Remember that voter intimidation—any form of harassment meant to influence or deter a person's vote—is against federal and most state laws. You can report voter intimidation to the Election Protection Hotline (1-866-OUR-VOTE) or the US Department of Justice Voting Section (800-253-3921).

THIS IS WHAT DEMOCRACY LOOKS LIKE!: MARCHES

When giant masses of people take to the streets, they create a visual impact that conveys in no uncertain terms: *this matters to us!* The amazing thing about protest marches is they really do change public opinion. And they also change the people who march. Gathering with hundreds—or thousands—of like-minded activists, chanting and shouting and speaking truth to power is exhilarating and often very moving. It can turn excitement into conviction, and conviction into a lifelong passion.

But here's a boring part: marches can be a bummer if you're cold and wet, or you have an asthma attack and didn't bring your inhaler.

So if you've got the go-ahead from your parents to attend a march, we've got some tips on how to make it fun, safe, and effective.

WHAT TO WEAR

Layers: You'll get hot. You'll get cold. You may even need to turn your hoodie into a pillow. Dress accordingly.

All that weather-appropriate stuff your parents are always trying to get you to put on: gloves, hats, a light down puffer. A rain poncho! You don't have to wear them, but bring them. Seriously, moms and dads knows what they're talking about.

Comfortable shoes or sneakers (or waterproof shoes if it's going to rain).

Glasses, not contacts: In the unlikely event that there's a confrontation involving airborne chemicals (like pepper spray), you'll want as much protection as possible for your eyes.

WHAT TO BRING

A clear backpack or a fanny pack: This is important. You really don't want to be schlepping a lot of crap, but there's stuff you'll need to bring. For security reasons, many towns and cities enforce the rule that all backpacks must be clear and no bigger than 17" x 12" x 6". Or, if you think you can travel very light, rock a cool fanny pack: 8" x 6" x 4" is the limit on "personal bags."

ID: Always a good idea.

Money: Not too much.

Sharpie: Just to be extra safe, it's a good idea to write some basic information (your name, emergency contact info, major allergies) on your arm.

Water bottle: Marches are often long and crowded and offer no access to refreshments. Water is essential!

Snacks: See above. Power Bars, beef jerky, dried fruit. Stuff that's easy to eat and easy to share.

Portable phone charger

Sunscreen

Small first aid kit

Regularly used medication

Menstrual products

Sign: These are fun, of course, but in a big crowd, signs can also be really helpful for keeping your group together. Save old gift wrapping tubes to mount your signs on. But check the organizers' site: some protests forbid dowels or poles.

Cacerolazo: A popular protest accessory in Latin countries, the "casserole" is basically a kitchen pot you bang with a wooden spoon. It's great for general noisemaking and will give your chants a beat to follow.

Bandanna: A multipurpose item for wiping your brow (or nose), cleaning up spills, or using as a flag. And if you moisten one with water, it can help protect your mouth and eyes from the above-mentioned noxious fumes.

WHAT TO DO

Don't go alone: It's not fun, and it's not safe, to go solo to a big march.

Have a safety plan: Because of the sheer volume of users, cell phones often don't work at large protests. Before you set off, make a plan in case you get separated from your group. Pick a landmark, a café, or if you've traveled from out of town, the place you're staying. If you're in a big group, use the buddy system.

Don't engage counter-protesters: It can be tempting to get into a shouting, or shoving, match with jerks on the other side. Don't. Seriously. It's not worth it.

March, chant, fight the patriarchy! Make your voice heard!

ARE YOU GOING TO TAKE THIS SITTING DOWN?: SIT-INS

Consider how almost sixty years ago, four college students sparked a movement that effectively ended segregation in the South, by sitting down. Believe it or not, sometimes one of the most powerful political statements you can make is to sit your butt down.

THE GREENSBORO FOUR START A MOVEMENT

In the winter of 1960, segregation was still the norm across the South. Many, if not most, restaurants, hotels, and stores refused to serve customers of color. On February 1, 1960, in Greensboro, North Carolina, four African American college students, Ezell Blair Jr., Joseph McNeil, Franklin McCain, and David Richmond, hatched a simple but powerful plan to protest segregation. They staged a sit-in at their local Woolworth lunch counter, which served only white patrons.

The Greensboro Four dressed formally, brought their textbooks and schoolwork with them, and spoke as politely as possible in the store. They knew they would not be served, but that wasn't the point. They planned the protest carefully and alerted the media beforehand: the idea was to showcase the irrationality and inhumanity of segregation. The four sat at the counter until closing time. The next day they came back with more students from local colleges, and a movement was born. Since 1960, people—young people particularly—have followed the same basic tenet as the Greensboro Four to stage sit-ins. Sit-ins are such a popular form of protest that even congressional members have used it. On June 22, 2016, more than 170 Democratic members of Congress, led by civil rights movement veteran Congressman John Lewis, staged a sit-in on the floor of the House of Representatives to protest a lack of legislative

action on gun control. The protest ended after one day, but it started a trend. Congressional Republicans have also staged sit-ins to push for offshore drilling legislation.

HOW TO STAGE YOUR OWN SIT-IN

FIGHT FOR A CAUSE THAT RESONATES WITH OTHERS

Maybe it is LGBTQIA rights or gun control, or maybe it is a travel ban or a local environmental issue, but chances are if it's really bothering you, it's probably making others upset as well.

GET PERMISSION FROM YOUR PARENTS

This is always a good idea when you're going to engage in public forms of activism, especially ones that may put you at odds with people in authority. At the very least, your parents should know where you are for safety reasons.

FIND A PLACE TO OCCUPY THAT IS SAFE BUT HAS HIGH VISIBILITY

The point is to bring attention to your cause, not to put people in danger, so find a spot that won't block emergency exits or vehicles or a general flow of movement that will inconvenience others.

GET THE WORD OUT

Make sure like-minded people know about your plans and are going to join you; the bigger the crowd, the more powerful the statement.

MAKE SURE YOU HAVE SUPPORT

You may need reinforcements, food, drinks, or replacement protesters for bathroom breaks. Have someone who is not an active part of the sit-in organize and run support.

ALERT THE MEDIA

Send out social media alerts and press releases about your plans. Notify local television and radio stations and newspapers.

BE POLITE AND RESPECTFUL

Perhaps the most important part of the Greensboro Four sit-in was their behavior toward those with whom they disagreed. They were peaceful and respectful at all times—even when other people jeered them or worse. As First Lady Michelle Obama said, "When they go low, we go high."

TURN YOUR BACK ON 'EM: WALKOUTS

Let's say a speaker at your graduation or assembly, or a speaker of the month at your school, university, or town hall, is someone with whom you strongly disagree, or even whom you consider to be *immoral*. What to do? WALK OUT! By organizing your friends and like-minded members of your community to stage a walkout you can make a silent but very powerful political statement in a coordinated and timely way.

2017 NOTRE DAME COMMENCEMENT

On Sunday, May 21, 2017, Vice President Mike Pence had just started his commencement address when about a hundred Notre Dame graduates stood up in their caps and gowns and silently walked out of the graduation ceremony in a single-file line. A packed stadium and national news crews, who were already filming, watched while many in the crowd both cheered and booed. Because many consider Notre Dame the most prominent Catholic university in the country and a place where conservative values are given a warm reception, the walkout was unexpected and therefore packed a bigger punch.

THINGS TO REMEMBER WHEN STAGING A WALKOUT

When at all possible, gather and organize like-minded people prior to the event. Sometimes speakers are a surprise, but if you know ahead of time who is coming, use it to your advantage! A walkout is a much more powerful statement than not attending at all.

VISUALS ARE IMPORTANT!

If possible, try to coordinate what you wear. A group that all wears the same T-shirts or color or hats is more noticeable.

LEAVE AT THE MOST IMPACTFUL TIME!

One reason the Notre Dame walkout on Vice President Pence was so noticeable was because the students filed out just as Pence started. Because the stadium was so large, the students proved a distraction for a significant portion of the speech.

STAY SILENT

If you are silent for your walkout, you are less likely to get in trouble or arrested for disrupting the event. Your actions will be unassailable.

GET THE WORD OUT!

Let the media know shortly before the event of your plans. Cameras rolling will help magnify your protest!

SIGNS OF CHANGE: PETITIONS

You probably think petitions are small potatoes, the kind of action more suited to getting rid of Styrofoam in the cafeteria than overthrowing the government. In fact, the right to petition is one of the most fundamental in our country. The colonists practiced it early and often, and the Founding Fathers guaranteed it in the First Amendment of the Constitution.

Petitions can be highly effective in achieving their cause because, in a democracy, NUMBERS count. And thanks to the internet, it's never been easier to gather those numbers. Organizations like Change.org and MoveOn.org offer simple methods for signing petitions or starting one of your own. Plus online communities like Facebook and Instagram make it super easy to draw attention to your cause. Nowadays the prospect of getting a hundred thousand signatures on a petition in a week is a very real possibility. And even if a given petition falls short of its ultimate goal, it can still succeed in galvanizing public opinion in a way that will eventually be impossible to ignore.

Here are just a couple of examples of successful modern-day petition campaigns:

BILL OF RIGHTS FOR SEXUAL ASSAULT SURVIVORS

In 2013, Amanda Nguyen was raped while she was a college student in Massachusetts. Disturbed by the lack of legal protections she was afforded, Amanda started a Change.org petition to have the rights of sexual assault survivors recognized by states individually and uniformly. She mobilized over 140,000 signatures on a petition and convinced Congress to pass the first-ever Sexual Assault Survivors' Bill of Rights in October 2016.

OVERTURNING THE BAN ON GAY SCOUTS

When Ryan Andresen was refused his hard-earned Eagle Scout award after his scoutmaster learned he was gay, Ryan's mother Karen swung into action. Her petition, to overturn the Boy Scouts of America's ban on gay scouts, drew almost five hundred thousand signatures. In May 2013, as a direct result of her efforts, the organization's national council reversed their policy.

#TAKEDOWNTHEFLAG

On June 17, 2015, nine African Americans were killed by a white supremacist while they were engaged in Bible study in a Charleston, South Carolina, church. In response, Karen Hunter began a MoveOn.org petition to have the Confederate flag, a potent symbol of the South's racist history, removed from in front of the South Carolina statehouse. The petition gathered more than five hundred thousand signatures. One day after the petition was delivered to Governor Nikki Haley, an announcement was made: the flag would come down.

HOW TO WRITE AND INITIATE A PETITION

Choose your cause and narrow your focus so that your cause resonates with others and will be more likely to gather high numbers of signatures. You can petition your school, corporations, and any level of local, state, or federal governments.

Utilize a petition website: Change.org, MoveOn.org, iPetitions.com, and Care2 (thepetitionsite.com) all have easy step-by-step instructions for writing, posting, and circulating a petition. Color of Change also uses petitions in its user-friendly campaign-making platform. The White House has its own petition website, We the People (petitions.whitehouse.gov). You will need one hundred thousand signatures within thirty days for the White House to officially review and respond, but we have faith in you!

Craft a compelling description and solicitation of your cause: Make it succinct and moving.

Test it out: Make sure your petition is easy to read, share, and sign.

ALEXANDRA STYRON

GET YOUR MOC WOKE: ENGAGING YOUR REPRESENTATIVES

When Barack Obama was elected president in 2008, a far-right faction of the Republican Party found their inner activist. They called themselves the Tea Party, in honor of, well, you get the joke. Conservative, mostly Christian, and mostly white, the Tea Partiers vowed to fight not only Democrats but even Republicans who supported legislation they didn't believe in, like more taxes, federally funded programs for the needy, flexible immigration laws: anything they considered "big government." To get the job done, this group took a page from the progressive playbook. They went local: training, coordinating, relying on grassroots organization, and pestering the hell out of their members of Congress.

And guess what? It worked. The Tea Party pretty much grabbed Washington by the throat. They fought every bit of legislation Obama presented, forced more moderate Republicans to reject compromise, and in the 2010 midterm elections, helped shift the House and Senate back to the right. After Obama won a second term, the Tea Party's obstructionism caused a complete government shutdown.

It's worth mentioning that a lot of the Tea Party's behavior was pretty awful: using bigoted language, burning political opponents in effigy, circulating misleading literature. In the end, they riled up their base with a lot of smack talk, convincing folks that only a leader working outside the system could do their bidding.

All of which brings us to 2018 and the really creepy episode of *American Horror Story* we're living now.

But if we truly want to turn this thing around, we have to take grassroots advocacy back from the Tea Party. We have to organize our friends, and they have to organize their friends. We need to establish some really clear goals.

And then go get our Members of Congress, or "MoCs," woke.

We should be all up in their business. Visiting with them, calling them, demanding town hall meetings. They're called representatives because *they work for us*. It's our job to let them know how we want them to govern.

So how do we do it?

Thanks to the cool people at Indivisible.org, we have a blueprint. Here's how to:

START A GROUP

Start a group dedicated to making your MoC aware of your opposition to the current administration's agenda. You could form a school club or reach out to kids in your general community.

Find some cofounders. Choose a few people who are equally enthusiastic but have different friend groups from you. This will help expand your reach and the makeup of the group.

Reach out via email, Instagram, or whatever method gets to the most people in your community or school.

Invite everyone who's interested to a kickoff meeting. You can assume that only 50 percent of the people who reply will actually show up, so aim high! Serve snacks. Play some music. Make it fun. At this meeting you're going to want to:

Manage the meeting. Try to keep everyone focused on your ultimate goal: applying pressure to your MoC to stop the administration's negative agenda. People will probably come to the meeting with a lot of emotions and a lot to say. That's great. Passion is powerful. But ultimately you'll need to stay on topic and establish a strategy.

Agree on a name—"Teens Against Tyranny," "Fight the Patriarchy," "Oh My God, What's Happening?!" Just some ideas . . .

Volunteer for roles. A lot will depend on how many people attend, but you should be able to place one or two people in charge of general coordination, and one or two people to track your congressperson's schedule, message, position, etc. Designate one person as the social media contact, and one or two people to work on getting your message out. (Maybe a member of your group has a parent who works in local media. Or someone has a blog that lots of people read. Get media interested in what you're doing!). Beyond that, you should find out who wants to make phone calls, host meetings, attend events, and record events. Make a roster and be sure everyone is copied when you distribute information.

Agree on a way to communicate. Facebook is really useful for these kind of groups, but you can use Google Groups or whatever works for you.

Expand! Ask everyone present to recruit several more members. Set goals for outreach. It's especially important to work toward diversity in your group. A diverse group spells inner strength and outer integrity.

MAKE CALLS

Mass phone calling is a great way to put pressure on your MoC, especially if it's difficult to meet with him or her in person. Tea Partiers flooded their congressional members' offices with phone calls and got noticed. Bigly.

Find your MoC's phone number at callmycongress.com.

Your group should pick a specific issue. A vote coming up, an issue you all care very much about, or any time-sensitive subject. One issue each time you call.

Find out whom you're talking to. Usually the person who answers the phone will be a junior staffer. Ask that person their name so you can greet them personally the next time you call. You should then ask for the legislative assistant in charge of the issue about which you are calling. If the staffer tells you the assistant is unavailable, ask to leave a voicemail message. Then follow up with an email. If you don't hear back, follow up again.

Here's what the emails look like:

> For Senate staff: StaffersFirstName_StaffersLastname@MoCsLastName.
> senate.gov.

> For House staff: StaffersFirstName.LastName@mail.house.gov.

Or you can go to house.gov/representatives/find and senate.gov/senators/contact to look up addresses.

Keep a record of your call. Take notes on what the staffer says. Everything they tell you is public information and can be shared widely. Compare your notes with others in the group in case of conflicting messages and answers.

Report back to your group and any media contacts your group has made.

SAMPLE CALL DIALOGUE

Calling strangers can be scary. It's easy to get nervous and forget what you wanted to say. Here's an example of how a conversation with your MoC's office might go:

> Staffer: Congressman Dweller O'Swamp's
> office. How can I help you?

You: Hi there, I'm a constituent of Congressman O'Swamp's. Can I please speak with the staffer who handles environmental issues?

Staffer: I'm happy to take down any comments you may have. May I ask for your name and address to verify you're in the congressman's district?

You: Sure thing. [Give name/address.] Can I ask whom I'm speaking with?

Staffer: Yes, this is Allie Gator.

You: Thanks, Allie! I'm calling to ask what the congressman is doing about President Trump's climate change–denying policies and his plans to roll back environmental protections. He already signed a bill that allows coal companies to dump mining water into streams. Now the EPA wants to kill the regulations on energy companies. I'm afraid these policies are going to speed up global warming, increase pollution, and make us all sick. What does Congressman O'Swamp think? And what's he doing about the proposed changes?

Staffer: Well, I really appreciate your concern. I can't speak for the congressman, but I can pass your concerns on.

You: Thanks, Allie, but I don't want you to just pass on my concerns. I'd like to know what's being done to stop this.

Staffer: Unfortunately there are a lot of other concerns at work when the congressman makes decisions.

You: Like what?

Staffer: Jobs. The economy.

You: What's more important than air and water? It's going to be hard to hold down a job if you can't breathe, don't you think? This is our future. Our planet. Why doesn't O'Swamp care about such fundamental issues?

Staffer: Well, I'm sure he'll be glad to hear your concerns.

You: I hope so. But in the meantime, I'll be telling my friends and family, and the press, that my representative is not doing his job representing us and is not responding to our concerns. Have a nice day.

Boom!

A WORD ABOUT INDIVISIBLE

After the election, a group of former Congressional aides sat down and wrote Indivisible, a guide for resisting the Trump agenda. They had seen firsthand how the Tea Party achieved their goals and knew the same thing could work in reverse. Without the lies and the hate and the fearmongering, of course. Since Indivisible was written, a lot of adults have put the plan into action, demanding time with their congressional representatives and sending them back to Washington with a clear set of directives. It totally works!

If adults can do it, you can, too. For more, check out Indivisible.org.

SCHOOL'S OUT, SERVICE IS IN: VOLUNTEERING, INTERNSHIPS, SUMMER PROGRAMS

When you care about social justice, it's a short leap to being of service to others. Most of you probably do nice things for people and animals and the planet all the time. Still, no book on activism would be complete without some information on volunteering and on more structured opportunities to work and learn. You may not get paid—actually, you may have to pay them!—but the value of the experience will be priceless.

As the great Mahatma Gandhi said, "the best way to find yourself is to lose yourself in the service of others."

VOLUNTEERING

Pick your thing: Do you want to help out at an animal shelter? Plant a community garden? Teach a child to read? Figure out what floats your boat!

Use your skill: Are you a knitter? Then maybe make blankets for hospitalized infants. Are you on the track team? Run a 5K to raise money for refugees. Play the guitar? Why not teach kids who don't have access to music lessons? Doing what you already know how to do can simplify volunteering, and make the experience even more fun.

Start small: No one's expecting you to give up all your free time. Offer your services once or twice and see how it goes. If you love it, you can add the activities to your routine. Just make sure you honor whatever commitment you make. People will be counting on you.

Buddy up: Take a friend or family member. Volunteering together can be a great way to spend time with people you love.

There are always plenty of places that need help in your community. But just in case, here are some national organizations to consider:

Best Buddies: A wonderful way to improve the lives of people with intellectual and developmental disabilities, Best Buddies will pair you with a new friend for social mentoring and rewarding experiences for you both. (bestbuddies.org)

Habitat for Humanity: This volunteer-based construction organization builds homes all over the world for people in need. They also sponsor student-initiated high-school chapters, offer summer programs, and convene week-long education and empowerment events for young people. All of that, and learning a useful skill too! (habitat.org)

Humane Society of America: One of the largest animal protection organizations in America, the Humane Society provides rescue services, runs shelters, and advocates for animal rights. People of all ages can find ways to volunteer. (humanesociety.org)

Meals on Wheels: Millions of homebound elderly people rely on Meals on Wheels for food delivery, companionship, and safety checks. Volunteer opportunities include meal preparation, delivery, social visits, and crafting. For some recipients, volunteers are the only face they see each day. Make yours one of them! (mealsonwheelsamerica.org)

SOCIAL JUSTICE LEARNING INSTITUTIONS / SUMMER PROGRAMS

ACLU Summer Institute: The ACLU's eight-day summer program in Washington, DC, is a cool opportunity to learn about civil rights, practice your debating skills, and get a feel for what it means to be a full-time social justice warrior. (aclu.org)

University of Pennsylvania Social Justice Research Academy: Part of the Penn Summer, this program offers an intensive curriculum focused on methods for battling inequality and injustice. Penn Summer also offers a precollege law program where you can start prepping to be the next Atticus Finch. (sas.upenn.edu/summer/programs/high-school)

Civic Leadership Institute: Offered at Johns Hopkins University (Baltimore, Md.) and Northwestern University (Chicago, Ill.), the Center for Talented Youth Civic Leadership Institute is a three-week service learning program that focuses on leadership education while encouraging participants to contribute to the betterment of their communities. (ctd.northwestern.edu, cty.jhu.edu)

One World Now!: This dynamic program is designed to educate and train the next generation of global leaders. Based in Seattle, One World Now! offers a school-year-long curriculum, as well as opportunities to study abroad, engage in their Global Youth Conference, and participate in workshops. One World Now! strives for inclusivity, especially for students of color and disadvantaged youth. (oneworldnow.org)

SENATE PAGE PROGRAM

Begun in 1829, the Senate Page Program offers a select group of high-school students the opportunity to see the wheels of government turn up close. Every year, thirty

pages are sponsored by their respective senators for either an academic semester or the summer session. Duties include delivering correspondence, preparing the Senate chamber for session, and—yes—making coffee. But for a senator! You must be sixteen years old and entering your junior year in high school. For more information, contact your senator's office. (senate.gov)

CAMPAIGN VOLUNTEERING

Some people get paid to work on political campaigns. But really the lifeblood of every candidate's team is the volunteers. Look, for instance, at the presidential campaign of Bernie Sanders. From a fringe candidacy run entirely by grassroots efforts, Bernie built one of the most exciting and galvanizing presidential efforts in decades.

So don't wait till the next presidential election. Find a local race, get in touch, and offer your time. Someone, probably another volunteer, will put you to work. Eventually you'll start identifying needs that are going unfilled, jobs that should be done. Don't wait to be asked or directed. Just do it! That's how campaigns work. They rely on the passion and initiative of volunteers. In a well-run campaign, everyone is welcome, no matter what your age or place in life. You'll make some new friends, learn a ton, and enjoy the camaraderie that can be found when you're doing something important with a group of like-minded people.

Your candidate might lose but, trust us, you won't!

DIY VACATION ACTIVISM

You could spend your spring break working on your tan. Or you could save your skin while you save the world! We like the idea of getting together with your family and/or a group of friends and creating a justice adventure. Help clean up a polluted riverbank, create a social media campaign, volunteer at Planned Parenthood. If you need ideas, or want to join a trip already in motion, check out alternativebreaks.org.

AND DON'T FORGET THE GAP YEAR!

Graduating from high school soon? Not sure you want to head straight to college? Talk to your parents about it, do some research, and decide if an "activist's gap year" is right for you.

Still not sure how to find your place? Check out volunteermatch.org. With volunteer networks in dozens of cities, this site can help you match your interests and age with volunteer opportunities near you.

FINANCIAL ACTIVISM, OR VOTING WITH YOUR WALLET

The Bad News: If you're under eighteen, you can't vote for candidates on Election Day.

The Good News: You can vote every day: with your wallet.

Financial activism is the practice of spending or withholding money based on socially responsible principles. It might be choosing Newman-O's, because the proceeds go to charity, over Oreos. Or it can mean boycotting the cosmetic company that engages in animal testing. Or it may refer to larger-scale divestment efforts, where you pressure institutions like your bank to stop investing in corporations that harm the environment. Basically it's a way of putting your money where your mouth is, and asking others to do the same.

As a young person, you're in a uniquely powerful position to make an impact. There are roughly forty-one million people between the ages of ten and nineteen in the United States and, according to research by Marketingvox/Rand, that group spends close to $259 billion every year on *stuff*.

So if money talks, you can say a lot.

SOCIALLY RESPONSIBLE SHOPPING

Buy products from companies that engage in corporate social responsibility, or CSR. Companies with high CSR ratings support good causes, are environmentally responsible, exhibit transparent and fair business practices, and treat employees with respect. Labels and packaging can often tell you if a product is

ECO-FRIENDLY
CRUELTY-FREE
SWEATSHOP-FREE
SOLD WITH THE PROMISE TO SHARE PROCEEDS
    WITH CHARITIES

Unfortunately, CSR doesn't come cheap. It costs more to pay your workers a living wage in the United States than to pay pennies to a child working in Thailand. It takes more real estate—and more infrastructure—to keep free-range chickens than to stuff all your egg-layers in a miserable pen. Companies that do the right thing often have a higher bottom line and they pass that cost on to you. So while it might not always be feasible for you to shop responsibly, it's something to aim for.

CONSUMING WISELY

Do I *really* need another pair of kicks? Maybe I could work a new look by shopping at the vintage store (especially the kind that supports charities!). That takeout place has awesome chimichangas. But the giant unrecyclable Styrofoam containers? Not so much.

It's an ongoing conversation we have with ourselves when we're trying to live ethically and mindfully. It takes more time, extra effort, and added patience to be a better citizen, but once you get in the habit, it will be hard to imagine ever going back.

BOYCOTTING

Boycotting is responsible *un*shopping. By denying an unethical company business, you negatively impact their brand, which in turn can force positive change.

Some of the greatest social progress in American history has been advanced through this form of protest. For example:

The Montgomery Bus Boycott: A year-long strike began in December 1955 when an African American woman named Rosa Parks refused to give up her seat to a white man on a segregated public bus. On December 20, 1956, the Supreme Court declared Alabama laws requiring buses to be segregated unconstitutional.

The Delano Grape Boycott: In 1965, Filipino American grape workers went on strike, demanding fair wages from California grape growers. They joined forces with the union group led by Cesar Chavez and Dolores Huerta. Together they formed United Farm Workers and continued the strike, which lasted more than five years and led to a widespread consumer boycott of non-union grapes. In 1970, the growers at last signed a contract with the UFW, benefitting more than ten thousand laborers.

The Nike Boycott: In the 1990s, the sports apparel company faced strong consumer pushback when it was revealed that many of their products were made in sweatshops under inhumane conditions. After years of consumer pressure and a global Nike boycott, the company made drastic changes in their business and labor policies. Nike is now considered a highly responsible and positive global brand.

Today, thanks to social media, boycotting as a form of activism has never been easier.

When President Trump enacted a travel ban from majority-Muslim companies, and Uber declined to join the yellow cab protest strike at New York airports,

#DeleteUber was born. The boycott resulted in the loss of hundreds of thousands of customers for Uber and exposed the car-hailing company to public scrutiny over several other bad business practices. And then there's Facebook, where, after United Airlines blatantly abused a passenger, more than fifteen thousand people swiftly signed onto a page calling for a boycott of the airline.

DO BOYCOTTS REALLY WORK?

Excellent question. In a word, yes. But it's a little tricky. While actions like the Montgomery Bus boycott and the grape boycott are considered undisputed success stories, experts warn that they can't be measured by financial activism alone. Both actions depended on a multitude of other factors, not least of which was really good timing. They were part of a continuum, building on legal strategies and other protest actions, within climates that were ripe for change. Not that that's bad news! Because we're living again in stormy times. And the more the wind blows, the larger the swell, and the higher the probability that you'll catch the crest of a change-making wave.

It does, however, take some moxie. Studies show that one of the greatest drags on a boycott's trajectory is willpower. For instance, you might have read about the decades-long boycott of Nestlé, for everything from unethical marketing of baby formula in developing countries to the deforestation of ele-phant habitats. So you swear off Kit Kats and Nerds, and you start a Facebook page to convince others to do the same. But, oh man, Nestlé also produces Sweet Leaf Tea. And PowerBars! And Lean Cuisine! And ~~Poland Spring!~~

Scratch that last one. Bottled water is an eco-nightmare no matter who produces it.

As Brayden King, a management professor at Northwestern University, has said, boycotts often fail because "it's just hard to actually stop buying a product that you're used to buying."

Here's another thing we want to be honest about. Even if you convinced the manager of your local Publix to clear every last Nestlé product off the shelves, the chance of making a dent in the company's revenue is infinitesimally slim.

So why boycott?

Because it isn't just about immediate sales. It's about reputation. A sustained boycott, aimed at a single firm and exposing unacceptable policies, can really damage a corporate brand. Once that happens, stock prices drop, valued employees go elsewhere, corporate partners flee. You've hobbled the company. And then you're in a position of power. Power to ask for specific concessions. Power to make change.

And that is something money can't buy.

SOCIALLY RESPONSIBLE INVESTING/DIVESTMENT

Socially responsible investing is about putting money into companies that behave in an ethical fashion. Divestment is taking money out of institutions that do business in a manner of which we don't approve.

One of the most famous and successful divestment campaigns began on American college campuses in the 1960s, but really got traction in the 1980s, and it helped to dismantle the brutal apartheid system in South Africa (for more on that effort, check out A Note from Me to You, page 1.) The college movement was just one of many important targeted efforts to bring about positive change in South Africa. Divestment was a key factor in bringing that country's racist political system to an end in the 1990s.

These days, a new divestment movement is gaining traction. Spearheaded by organizations like 350.org and Divest-Invest Philanthropy, this campaign seeks broad divestment from the fossil fuel industry. Supporters of the movement believe that the most efficient way to combat climate change is to cut our dependence on the use of coal and oil and gas that's fueling it.

Many universities, banks, religious institutions, and pension funds invest heavily in fossil fuels. So, to join in the divestment campaign, you can:

Do your banking at a fossil-fuel-free bank. And ask your parents to join you!

Speak with your clergy about your interest in the issue. See if they can help you research the investments made by your place of worship and ask them to partner with you on working for change.

Talk with your parents about making clean energy choices for your family's home.

Get your science teacher to join you in petitioning for a fossil-fuel-free teachers' pension fund in your town or city.

Join the Fossil Fuel Divestment Student Network on Facebook. Get involved now and be primed to join the divestment forces on college campuses.

How you spend your money—or don't—can have a real impact on so many of the issues you care about. And the internet is there to help you figure out how. Goodguide .com, fairtradeusa.org, and grabyourwallet.org are great places to start. Or check out some apps, like Buycott, Good On You, and Green Globe.

SOCIAL ENTERPRISE

Social or entrepreneurial activism is about combining profit-making businesses with worthy social causes.

Or, as some people say, "doing well by doing good."

There are a few different ways to approach social enterprise. The simplest method is producing goods and giving a portion of the proceeds to charity.

For example, suppose you design, produce, and sell a T-shirt with a funky chicken on it and donate 10 percent of your profit to the ACLU. That's cool.

Or how about for every five chicken shirts you sell, you buy an egg-laying hen for a hungry family through an organization like Oxfam or Heifer International? That's cool, too.

Or what if you make a T-shirt with a funky chicken on it and apply for a fellowship to grow your company so that you sell lots of shirts, and donate whole flocks so that people in developing countries can raise their own chickens and feed themselves. That's also very cool!

Really, any way you go about making money and giving back is excellent. And no one says you have to be completely selfless about it (though that's a nice idea). If you have a million-dollar idea and can make the world a better place while putting some money in your own pocket, more power to you. Take, for instance, Mikaila Ulmer, who started selling her Me & the Bees Lemonade when she was only five years old, secured a $60,000 investment from *Shark Tank* at nine, and is now able to give thousands of dollars annually to help save the global bee population. Or Kenton Lee, who was just out of college when a visit to an African orphanage inspired his invention of durable sandals that adjust up several sizes for needy children. Or Kenneth Shinozuka, who created a motion-activated sensor that helps caregivers track the movements of Alzheimer's patients like his grandfather. All young people, making money and making nice. That's how it works. As long as you're sharing what you make, you're engaging in social enterprise.

SO YOU WANT TO BE AN ENTREPRENEURIAL ACTIVIST?

Here are eight tips to keep in mind.

ARTICULATE YOUR MISSION: Like all good enterprises, yours should begin with a clearly stated mission. If you're passionate, the agenda should be easy to formulate. You recognize a problem and you're setting out to fix it.

A GOOD PRODUCT ADVANCES A GOOD MISSION: Are you going to make Cloud Cookies for Climate Change? They better be the best cloud cookies—whatever that is—anyone has ever tasted. And they'll need to be priced to sell while still turning a profit. Bottom line: your entrepreneurial mission is a business. Run it like one.

ENGAGE A LIKE-MINDED AUDIENCE: You will need the support of people who care about your mission as much as you do. If you can engage them, you'll have a much better chance at a successful launch. Have you designed cute dog hats for sale that can also be given to shelters to make adoptable pups irresistible-looking? Then work with your local pet store to set up a table out front and show them off. Contact the ASPCA and offer to donate a pile of hats in exchange for a feature on their website. Put one on your own mutt and bring him to the church picnic. Find other animal lovers and spread the word.

ASK FOR ADVICE: Don't be afraid to ask for help. People with business experience are usually quite happy to share their knowledge. And if they're good at what they do, that probably means they've made a pretty good living at it. Plus, if you ask for advice and apply it, you might find those same people may be willing to make an investment in what you're doing.

TRY CROWDFUNDING: Using crowdfunding sources like Indiegogo and Kickstarter is a really good way to meet your start-up goals and connect with your grassroots audience. A good crowdfunding campaign takes work! But if you have a strong idea and a noble mission, anything is possible. (If you're under eighteen, you'll need to get consent from an adult to crowdfund.)

SEEK OUT THE EXPERTS: Social enterprise is a fast-growing field, and there are lots of organizations out there that want to help budding entrepreneurs. Check out Ashoka (ashoka.org), the Skoll Foundation (skoll.org), the Social Enterprise Greenhouse (segreenhouse.org), and other like-minded organizations to see what kind of support is available for people like you.

BORROW MONEY, BUT BE PREPARED TO PAY IT BACK: At the end of the day, you may have to borrow money from people you know. If it's not your parents, then get their permission to ask others. You've got a great idea and can likely make dough on it. But make sure your business plan includes a way to pay people back.

SOCIAL MEDIA: Tweet me, like me, follow me on Insta. You know the drill. Once your idea has come together, shout it from the rooftops. Don't be shy. Be proud and be pushy.

HOW TO ASSESS THE NEWS

In 1835, the *New York Sun* ran a series of articles detailing the discovery of life on the moon. With the purported aid of a new super-telescope, astronomers were said to have seen bearded blue unicorns, bipedal beavers, and giant "man-bats" frolicking through lush forests and on pebble-strewn beaches. And though the *Sun*'s nonsense was eventually debunked, false stories about extraterrestrial life have remained a staple of tabloids for centuries.

Still, vetting the news didn't truly become tricky until the rise of the internet at the end of the last century. While your parents once got their news primarily from three network channels and local or national newspapers, the web suddenly produced an endless stream of information. Cyberspace—a cheap, easy, and basically lawless place to say stuff—has encouraged a Wild West kind of mentality when it comes to news. And the danger of such recklessness was never more apparent than during the "shoot 'em up" election won by Donald Trump.

Spurred on by ugly campaign rhetoric and a polarized electorate, yellow (meaning illegitimate) journalism flourished during the 2016 campaign. Teenagers in the Eastern European country of Macedonia got rich writing Trump-friendly clickbait, while Democrat-friendly sites peddled photos that claimed to reveal Mike Pence's "gay past." And of course, there were all those Russians trolling voters at every turn. Mostly, it was junk news that stirred up emotions and probably swayed some minds. But then, in December 2016, a man named Edgar Welch drove to Washington, DC, armed with an AR-15 assault-style rifle. He had read online that presidential candidate Hillary Clinton was running a child sex ring out of a pizza parlor and was intent on breaking it up John Wick–style.

Yes. That actually happened.

These days, beyond the real physical consequences of spreading fake news, another problem has popped up. Since his inauguration, President Trump has persisted in labeling any story he doesn't like "fake news." Thoroughly researched, verifiable stories from trusted news sources like *The New York Times*, *The Washington Post*, CNN, and *The Wall Street Journal*, organizations that play a crucial role in our democracy and have, collectively, hundreds of years of honest reporting under their belt. But a lot of people believe what the president says, so they no longer trust the press. The end result: it's increasingly hard to tell truth from lies. Whom can you trust?

For some answers, we turned to a professional: Staci Baird, a journalist and professor of communications at the University of La Verne in California.

Professor Staci Baird tells us how to craft a "News Diet Plan"

Create a proactive plan for news consumption, or a "news diet." Think about the kinds of stories and sources of news you consume. If all you read is TMZ (not that you would!), you're missing out on the important stories that impact your life and your community. And it's not just about cutting things out, but about what you add. Well-respected news sources—papers with wide circulation or major TV channels—are really good supplements to your daily information intake.

If you aren't familiar with a particular source, read about it on Wikipedia. Wikipedia is a great resource that can tell you about a publication's owners and country of origin; this could provide clues to further understanding the framing of a particular story. However, Wikipedia should also be read with a skeptical eye. A good wiki article will have footnotes that can be traced to original sources.

Read the About page of a website. It will tell you who is behind a particular publication, and also what their goals are. Many satire sites are upfront about their desire to entertain with humorous twists on the news, and may say that they are "for entertainment purposes only." But not all satire sites are so forthcoming. Those are the ones you have to beware of!

Reporters often joke, "If your mom says she loves you, check it out." So before you go sharing articles, think about this:

Some stories will be entirely made up (think satire), for example, "*Tyrannosaurus rex* Discovered Living in Central Park." You'll know it's fake because it sounds so outrageous.

Some stories will be partially based on facts; they may even quote real studies or sources. However, the studies or sources are usually taken out of context and distort the truth. For example, in June 2017, a pro-Trump group used President Obama's voice out of context in a radio ad for Georgia's special election (www.cnn.com/2017/06/18/politics/kfile-obama-georgia-ad/index.html).

Some stories will be mostly true, but the information may be outdated. Always check the date the story was published.

It's important to keep in mind that many stories will only present one side of an issue. The key is to look for stories that represent multiple viewpoints, providing a fair and balanced look at an issue. This is what real journalism strives to do.

Looking for more ways to get and vet your news? The smart people at Common Sense Media (commonsensemedia.org) recommend these four excellent sites:

Poynter.org: for solid news journalism and accessing tools for fact checking.

OpenSecrets.org: a site where you can see how money is playing a role in politics.

FactCheck.org: Wondering if a politician's claims are really true? Check it here.

Snopes.com: A great site to get urban myths debunked, and crazy-but-true stories confirmed.

SOCIAL MEDIA ACTIVISM

In the last twenty years, almost every aspect of our lives has been transformed by the World Wide Web. You name it, it's been virtualized. And while you could argue that, in some ways, the digital era has complicated our lives, it has made lots of what we do easier and better. Activism is one of those things.

Social media has become a valuable tool in the defense of human rights all over the globe. But here in the United States, where access is unrestricted and speech is free, the impact has been especially profound. In 2011, the Occupy Wall Street protest was largely mobilized by Facebook and Twitter. In 2013, the hashtag #BlackLivesMatter ignited an urgent national conversation about race. In 2017, the #MeToo hashtag became a powerful way to unite the voices of women who have experienced sexual assault and harassment. Every second of the day, someone is using their feed to expose a wrong, celebrate a right, agitate for change, or mess with powerful people in amusing and creative ways.

FACEBOOK

Yeah, yeah, we know. Facebook is for old people. But it's also an insanely popular site—over two billion monthly users, more than one billion of whom log on daily—and the single best way to communicate, network, find a group, or start one of your own. Virtually every successful nonprofit has a Facebook page now, and you can hardly run a political campaign or a charity 5K anymore without being expected to post updates for your friends and supporters. You want people to like your initiatives? They need to like you on Facebook!

THE WOMEN'S MARCH

On November 8, 2016, Donald Trump was elected the forty-fifth president of the United States. A lot of people were shocked by the outcome—and not too happy, either. That night, a woman in Hawaii, Teresa Shook, posted on the Pantsuit Nation Facebook page "I think we should march." *By the next morning, ten thousand people had signed up.*

Meanwhile, on the other side of the country, a fashion designer named Bob Bland was working on the same idea. The two women quickly joined forces and brought onboard three seasoned organizers: Tamika Mallory, Linda Sarsour, and Carmen Perez (see page 124). By the third week of November, the Women's March on Washington, scheduled for the day after Trump's inauguration, was a viral sensation.

Of course, not everyone could make it to Washington. But guess what? They marched anyway. They marched in Philly and in LA. They marched in Wichita and in Denver. They marched in Brussels and Nairobi and Tokyo. They marched in Anchorage and Antarctica!

On January 21, 2017, nearly five million people of all genders and ages around the globe took to the streets to protest bigotry, misogyny, climate change denial, and just about every other wretched element that had infused the new president's campaign. More than half a million people marched in DC alone. It was a much bigger action than anyone anticipated.

In fact, it was the biggest one-day protest in US history.

INSTAGRAM

If a picture is worth a thousand words, an Instagram account can speak volumes. Sharing well-curated images about a specific theme is a great way to raise awareness for your issue. For instance, the actress Emma Watson frequently posts photographs of clothing made by socially responsible designers in order to promote sustainable fashion. But you don't have to be a movie star to get into the act. Photographer Paul Nicklen uses his Instagram account to celebrate the beauty of polar regions and reveal the effects of global warming. Amber Amour uses hers to raise awareness about sexual assault. And with an added hashtag (more on that in a minute) #StopRapeEducate, she's inviting the growth of her movement through a participatory campaign. Instagram can also be a great venue for artivism (more on that in a minute), combining the aesthetics of photography with the force of messaging.

TWITTER

What started as a platform for random blurting has, over the last decade, become a singular tool for the expression of ideas and the dissemination of knowledge.

Some people just can't get enough of it!

Attaching a word or phrase to a hashtag (#) helps bring awareness to an issue by creating a reusable title and allowing viewers to search through a shared database. #IStandWithAhmed— named for fourteen-year-old Ahmed Mohamed, who was arrested when a teacher thought his homemade clock was a bomb—has drawn lasting attention to Islamophobia. And, in 2014, the fatal shooting of Michael Brown by police in Ferguson, Missouri, prompted the tweeting of #Ferguson more than twenty-seven million times. You can also get creative with a hashtag. Attach one to your senator's name, or to the president, and see if you can get some attention!

P.S. Hashtags work great, but don't forget about the @ reply feature. Along with retweets, it's a great way to engage other Twitter users who share your values and ideas.

BLOGS AND WEBSITES

Creating your own website or blog (a blog *is* a website, a simple one) will definitely be more of a commitment than the occasional tweet or Instagram post. It's the difference between inviting people to picnics on sunny days and opening a restaurant. Once you've built up followers for your website, they will come expecting to be served frequent, new content. And that can end up feeling like a lot of pressure. The upside is you have a multidimensional forum, with no real restrictions, for presenting information, opinions, and links to other content. Blogs are great for recording your experiences and opinions in prose and photos. Maybe you intend to spend the summer working as a volunteer for an immigration organization? A daily blog diary will offer others a critical window into the real world through your anecdotal experience. If you come home and decide you want to start an organization to help other teenagers connect with underserved populations, then an expanded website will be an excellent second step. (For example, check out FirstHereThenEverywhere.org, a website for youth activists founded by Chloe Maxmin.)

Another great thing about websites is you can sell stuff on them. If you've designed a T-shirt with a clever message, or you want to raffle off your troll collection to raise funds for Greenpeace, you'll be able to advertise and manage your wares there.

Here are the basics steps to get you started:

Come up with a name (Stealthiscountry.com is taken. Sorry ☺).

Pick a platform, like Squarespace, Wix, or WordPress.

Choose a domain name and a web host (Bluehost, HostPapa, there are lots).

Set up your blog on your host site.

Customize your look with a cool design.

Get posting!

For more tips on how to be a social media activist, check out these sites: socialbrite.org, blmactivism.com, and howto.informationactivism.org.

PROTECTING YOUR PRIVACY ON THE INTERNET

These days, the internet is a huge part of activism, whether it's finding out where the protest is, sending around online petitions, or responding to the president's dumb tweets. But the internet can be a dangerous place, with hackers and trolls roaming around ready to pounce. Here are some tips for keeping yourself safe while fighting the good fight through social media:

Use a password manager: Can you remember all your passwords? (Or do you have only one for everything?) That probably means they're simple enough to be easy to crack. Saved all your passwords in a Word document, the Notes app or other un-encrypted form? Then they're not secure! Software like 1Password and Dashlane protects your passwords, can generate randomized passwords, and organizes them so you don't have to remember all those wacky random numbers and letters.

Use two-factor authentication: Google, Facebook, Twitter, and Tumblr all allow you to enable a two-step verification process when you log in. Usually this means a service will ask for not only your password but also a code that's been sent to a separate, trusted device. So, even if someone has your password, without your phone, they can't get into your account.

Pay attention to your privacy settings: You should only be sharing info with friends and family. On that note, don't accept friend requests from people you don't know.

Use a VPN: Virtual private networks (VPNs) are tools you can install to encrypt the traffic coming from your device and mask your internet Protocol (IP) address. Unfortunately you usually have to pay for VPNs, and not all of them are created equal; in fact, some are a little sketchy. PureVPN, IPVanish, and NordVPN are a few of the well-known and trusted VPNs, but do your own research!

Turn off geotagging: A lot of apps and social media sites use geotagging to mark when and where your posts come from. Geotagging attaches location data (literally latitude and longitude) to pictures, videos, Snapchats, or Facebook status updates. This can be kind of cool, but also kind of dangerous, since your location information can easily get into the hands of someone you didn't intend it to.

Update your software regularly: Hackers often attack known weakness in soft-ware that companies have long since fixed. If you keep your operating system and web browser updated, you'll be less vulnerable.

For texting, use Signal, especially when texting about organizing and protests: Signal is a messaging app that doesn't collect your data, so the company can't turn it over to the government.

Think about what you're posting: This stuff isn't totally foolproof, so even with all these protections, it's important to really think about what you put on the internet or communicate digitally.

FAMILY MATTERS: TALKING TO RELATIVES YOU DISAGREE WITH

Yep, you're right. The blame for our current situation most likely lands on the shoulders of people older than you. And what's worse is, you may even be related to some of them! What's the old adage? *You can't choose your family . . .*

AARGH! MY (INSERT NAME OF LOVED ONE HERE) VOTED FOR TRUMP!!!!

It's a drag, we know, when people in your own family don't agree with you politically. You wonder how anyone you know and love could possibly have voted for someone you consider to be *unacceptable*. And how are you supposed to talk to them at Thanksgiving, or on a daily basis? Well, here is the hard truth: to take back this country peacefully and respectfully, we are going to need to understand why it was hijacked in the first place, and as difficult as that may seem, sometimes the best place to start the process is with those closest to us. So here is a step-by-step guide for how to talk to your grandparents, parents, other relatives, or even friends (!) who don't agree with you politically.

PRACTICE GOOD LISTENING

We know, we know, all you want to do is start shouting, "What is *wrong* with you?" but try to remember why you are having this conversation in the first place. You need to try to understand where your relative or friend is coming from, and the best way to do that is to listen. Perhaps you could start the conversation by saying: "Wow, there is so much that upsets me about candidate X, what is it that you like about him?"

DON'T TRY TO CHANGE ANYONE'S MIND

Dr. Jamie M. Howard, a clinical psychologist at the Child Mind Institute in New York City, recommends acknowledging from the outset that you are not going to change Grandpa's mind. Instead, you should think of the conversation as a *sharing of ideas*. It's kind of like a school science project: you need to adopt a research mind-set.

DON'T ATTACK

Again, as much as you may want to hurl insults at your loved one, this approach will not work or help! Keep your cool, stay calm, and don't say anything mean or personal.

PULL THE PLUG IF IT ISN'T GOING WELL

If things get too heated or uncomfortable on either end, try to wrap things up quickly and gracefully. Instead of saying, "Let's agree to disagree," try: "You have given me a lot to think about here, but how about if we talk about something else now?"

REMEMBER THAT FAMILY IS IMPORTANT

Yes, politics are important and can potentially have life-or-death implications, but family is important, too. In general, political disagreements are not worth walking away from a loved one. Before or after a political conversation with someone you disagree with, Dr. Howard recommends to trying to "hold on to your positive impressions of the important people in your life." You may not agree with your grandmother about a given candidate or issue, but you still love her brownies! In most cases, it is still possible to derive love, comfort, and support from relatives and friends with whom you disagree politically.

For more on tough talk and tough conversations, check out "Speak Up: Responding to Everyday Bigotry" on the Southern Poverty Law Center's website (splcenter.org).

Maggie Gyllenhaal

Maggie Gyllenhaal is known for her roles in such films as *The Dark Knight*, *Donnie Darko*, *Crazy Heart*, *Nanny McPhee Returns*, and *Secretary*. She received a Golden Globe for her role in the miniseries *The Honourable Woman*. Maggie lives in Brooklyn, New York, with her husband (actor Peter Sarsgaard) and their two daughters.

I think it's amazing the lengths people will go to not to look at the truth, especially when it's painful. Teenagers are often amazing beacons of truth, seeing right through the strange ways that adults protect themselves from painful things. To me, it's obvious (but terrifying) that we're in a moment of crisis. We *must* change the way we're living; we must consider our effect on the world we're all sharing. And the first step is to *talk* about it, truthfully, clearly, often. Talking about the truth is always a relief. And it helps us organize our ideas into manageable action. I think that's the way to be an activist. To keep your eyes wide open, looking for what YOU think is right and what *you* think is wrong. And to talk about it. So in our family, we read the news every day. We talk about it all day long. We go to marches and meetings. I write essays about what's important to me. I make movies about what's impor-

tant to me. We recycle and compost. We drive an electric car. We live off the grid up in the country. We share some of what we have with people who need it. We support news sources that help us stay informed. And we keep a lookout for new ways to be helpful and fight for what we feel is important.

GET CREATIVE!

Harnessing your creativity to say something meaningful is an exciting pursuit. Doing it well is really hard. But when you connect with an audience by surprising, moving, provoking, or amusing them, it's a total thrill. When you speak to people's hearts, you have the power to expand their minds.

So let's talk about . . .

ARTIVISM

The artists whose comics introduce each of the issues in "The What" are practicing artivism. They are marrying their conscience to their creative work, just like Talib Kweli when he raps about police shootings or Lena Dunham when she challenges gender roles in her writing and acting. As the writer and performer Eve Ensler (*The Vagina Monologues*, *The Good Body*) describes it, artivism is "a kind of escalated passion . . . [that] has all the ingredients of activism, but is charged with the wild creations of art." It is, she says, "where edges are pushed, imagination is freed, and a new language emerges altogether."

VISUAL ARTS

Picasso made protest art. So did Max Ernst. And Judy Chicago and Gordon Parks. Now we have Ai Weiwei and Kara Walker and Banksy and Shepard Fairey. All artists playing with history and imagery, and upending expectations, to make powerful statements and awe-inspiring art. If you're a painter, a sculptor, a photographer, or any kind of artist, you've got an opportunity to say something with your work.

ZINES

Got an idea? Something you want to get off your chest? The world is waiting for your zine! All you need is pens, paper, and a copy machine. With roots in the old-fashioned political pamphlet, zines took off as a form of DIY publishing in the late twentieth century, becoming identified particularly with Riot Grrrl, an influential feminist punk movement and music scene of the 1990s. Of course, today's technology has made it possible to create much more sophisticated products, and some zines have moved to websites. But the rough look of homemade zines is a big part of their radical power and continued popularity.

MUSIC

Is there any medium that brings people together like music? What else can bind a crowd in passion, anger, and determination like a protest song? From the World War I–era ditty "I Didn't Raise My Boy to Be a Soldier" to Woody Guthrie's "This Land Is Your Land" to "We Shall Overcome," on up to Beyoncé's "Freedom," American musicians have been belting out tuneful oppositions to war and injustice for forever. Those anthems can power a generation bent on change.

What's your garage band singing about? Well then, get to it!

20 GREAT PROTEST SONGS

"This Land Is Your Land": Woody Guthrie
"Strange Fruit": Billie Holiday
"We Shall Overcome"
"If I Had a Hammer (Hammer Song)": Pete Seeger and Lee Hays
"Masters of War": Bob Dylan
"A Change Is Gonna Come": Sam Cooke
"Mississippi Goddam": Nina Simone
"Universal Soldier": Buffy Sainte-Marie
"Ohio": Crosby, Stills, Nash & Young
"The Revolution Will Not Be Televised": Gil Scott-Heron
"What's Going On": Marvin Gaye
"Get Up, Stand Up": Bob Marley
"Sunday Bloody Sunday": U2
"Meat Is Murder": The Smiths

"The Message": Grandmaster Flash and the Furious Five
"Fight the Power": Public Enemy
"Rebel Girl": Bikini Kill
"Killing in the Name": Rage Against the Machine
"Alright": Kendrick Lamar
"Hell You Talmbout": Janelle Monáe

FILM AND VIDEO

Since the dawn of cinema, thousands of movies have been made that shine a light on the darkest corners of humanity, the ones that most need illuminating. There are dramas, documentaries, satires, movies inspired by historic movements, and movies *about* historic movements. Some of these films are old and epic and cost a zillion dollars to make and some were made on a shoestring but ended up having an outsize impact on our consciousness, like the 2017 film *Get Out*, for instance.

Lucky for you, today's cheap and easy digital technology means anyone with a point of view and a little imagination can make a film and post it instantly for the world to see.

Now, doing it well is a whole other thing. But you know that. The best way to learn about making movies with a message is to watch them. Here are a few to start with.

10 GREAT POLITICAL FILMS

The Battle of Algiers
12 Angry Men
Norma Rae
Network
Silkwood
Do the Right Thing
Philadelphia

Erin Brockovich
Dear White People
Get Out

LITERATURE

If you have a social conscience, and you want to be a writer, there are plenty of ways to practice your craft. You can write for the student newspaper, or pen essays and post them on a blog. You can submit an op-ed to your local paper. Or take what you know and turn it into art, as poets and novelists do.

10 CLASSIC POLITICAL NOVELS

The Grapes of Wrath by John Steinbeck
Native Son by Richard Wright
1984 by George Orwell
Animal Farm by George Orwell
Giovanni's Room by James Baldwin
Fahrenheit 451 by Ray Bradbury
The Chocolate War by Robert Cormier
The Color Purple by Alice Walker
The Handmaid's Tale by Margaret Atwood
Americanah by Chimamanda Ngozi Adichie

THEATER AND PERFORMANCE

The theater of protest has a long and rich history. Rabble-rousers. Clowns. Street theater. Guerrilla theater. Epic theater. Agitprop. Kabuki. With text or without. Completely

masked or thoroughly naked. The one-woman show. The flash mob. Emma Sulkowicz even did their 2014 Columbia University senior thesis as a protest piece. Their performance, "Carry That Weight" (shown here), was a response to their campus sexual assault case.

If you are staging an act with a political message, the variations are endless, and the effects potentially devastating—in a good way!

10 GREAT POLITICAL PLAYS

The Children's Hour by Lillian Hellman
Mother Courage and Her Children by Bertolt Brecht
The Crucible by Arthur Miller
A Raisin in the Sun by Lorraine Hansberry
Hair by Galt MacDermot
For colored girls who have considered suicide | when the rainbow is enuf
  by Ntozake Shange
Real Women Have Curves by Josefina López
Angels in America by Tony Kushner
The Laramie Project by Moisés Kaufman and the Tectonic Theater Project
Hamilton by Lin-Manuel Miranda

CULTURE JAMMING

As a form of protest art, culture jamming is pretty interesting. It aims to subvert the messages of existing media by altering them. When you turn an image or slogan on

its head, so to speak, you're commenting on what that image or slogan is trying to say. In doing so, you're exposing bad business practices, greed, hypocrisy, injustice. Culture jamming is a form of social commentary and also a kind of art. For instance, this . . .

AND THIS . . .

AND THIS!

GLOSSARY

Appropriation
when something is inappropriately, disrespectfully, and without permission taken from another culture

Assimilate
when an individual or group, by force, motivation, or choice, erases their own cultural background or beliefs in order to adopt those of the ruling class and be normalized in society

Biodegradable
naturally breaks down without harming the planet

Bisexual
experiencing sexual attraction to their own gender and other genders

Carcinogenic
cancer-causing

Cisgender
often shortened to "cis," refers to someone who identifies with the sex they were assigned at birth; opposite of transgender

Deportation
forcible removal from a nation or sovereign state due to lack of citizenship

Displacement
when an individual, family, or community is forced to uproot and move to another place (whether slowly, bit by bit, or all at once) due to gentrification, globalization, colonization, warfare, or some other socioeconomic condition; often the reason for immigration

DREAM Act (Development, Relief, and Education for Alien Minors)
legislation passed by the Obama administration that would allow people who immigrated to the United States as minors to get green cards, Social Security numbers, work permits, and driver's licenses, and create a path toward permanent residency

Environmental racism
when people of color are subjected to hazardous situations because of their devaluation in society

Feminism
people sometimes joke that feminism is "the radical belief that women are human beings." That's actually not so far off. Most broadly, feminism refers to the belief in and struggle for gender equality

Fossil fuels
fuels formed through the natural decay of ancient organisms; oil, natural gas, coal, and petroleum are all fossil fuels

Gender
generally sex is based on biological, anatomical, and physiological characteristics, while gender is based on personal identity, such as male, female, or somewhere along the spectrum

Globalization
the increasing global interconnectedness of economies, cultures, and political systems driven by the rise of transportation and communications technologies. Often critiqued due to the unequal power relationships among countries, and how some countries suffer from economic, political, and cultural domination of the most developed nations.

Green card
authorization given to noncitizens to live and work in the United States

Hijabi
a Muslim who wears one of the different forms of Islamic veils: hijab is a general term, but can also specifically refer to a head covering that leaves the face clear while covering the head and neck; a niqāb covers the head, neck, and face, but leaves the eyes clear; a burqa is a full-body veil that covers the entire face, with a mesh screen over the eyes through which the wearer can see out

ALEXANDRA STYRON

Homophobia
irrational fear of and hatred toward LGB people

Interfaith
productive, cooperative exchange among people and communities of different faiths

Intersectionality
the way that social categories, such as race, gender, and class, combine, overlap, or intersect, especially within marginalized groups

Intersex
refers to a number of conditions in which someone is born with reproductive anatomy or sex characteristics that don't fit with typical notions of male or female

Islamophobia
irrational fear of and hatred toward Muslim people

Latinx
a gender-neutral term used to refer to people of Latin American descent

LGBTQIA
Lesbian, Gay, Bisexual, Transgender, Questioning (or Queer), Intersex, Asexual (not experiencing sexual attraction or desire; can also stand for Allies)

Marginalization
a practice that excludes, denies power to, or treats a group of people as less important

Misogyny
a deep-seated, learned prejudice against women

Nationalism
patriotism taken to the extreme, centered around a belief in the superiority of one's country over others

Naturalization
when an immigrant is made a citizen of their new country of residence; may be by a variety processes

Patriarchy
a system of male domination, driven by misogyny

Queer
an umbrella term used to refer to people who are not heterosexual and/or cisgender; preferred by many people because it rejects binaries and is inclusive

Rape culture
a culture that devalues women and their agency to the point that sexual violence is implicitly condoned and normalized

Renewable resources
unlike fossil fuels, resources like solar, wind, and hydropower that are not depleted with use and can be replenished over time

Sikhs
practitioners of a religion with origins in the Indian subcontinent whose turbaned adherents are often mistaken for Muslims and subjected to Islamophobia

Suffrage
the right to vote

Sustainable
refers to practices that don't have a negative impact on the environment and/or that use resources without depleting them in the long term

Systemic
spread throughout a system, or affecting the entire system, as in racism throughout the legal system of our country

Title IX
a law passed in 1972 which says that no one may, on the basis of their sex, be excluded from participation in, denied the benefits of, or be subjected to discrimination under any educational program that receives federal funding

Transgender
refers to someone who does not identify with the sex they were assigned at birth

Transphobia
irrational fear of and hatred toward transgender people

WANT TO KNOW MORE?

OUR ARTISTS

Roz Chast: rozchast.com
GB Tran: gbtran.com
Nicole Georges: nicolejgeorges.tumblr.com
Marguerite Dabaie: mdabaie.com
Richie Pope: richiepope.com
Liz Prince: lizprincepower.com
Jensine Eckwall: jensineeckwall.com

CLIMATE CHANGE

Books

The End of Nature. Bill McKibben. Random House, 2006.
Generation Green: The Ultimate Teen Guide to Living an Eco-Friendly Life. Linda Sivertsen and Tosh Sivertsen. Simon Pulse, 2008.
Going Blue: A Teen Guide to Saving Our Oceans, Lakes, Rivers, & Wetlands. Cathryn Berger Kaye and Philippe Cousteau. Free Spirit Publishing, 2010.
It's Getting Hot in Here: The Past, Present, and Future of Climate Change. Bridget Heos. HMH Books for Young Readers, 2016.
This Changes Everything: Capitalism vs. The Climate. Naomi Klein. Simon & Schuster, 2014.
Tracking Trash: Flotsam, Jetsam, and the Science of Ocean Motion. Loree Griffin Burns. HMH Books for Young Readers, 2010.
Walden. Henry David Thoreau. Ticknor and Fields, 1865.
We Are the Weather Makers: The History of Climate Change. Tim Flannery, adapted by Sally M. Walker. Candlewick, 2010.

Documentaries

Chasing Ice. Jerry Aronson, producer. 2012.
Climate of Doubt. Catherine Upin, Raney Aronson and Missy Frederick, producers. 2012.
The 11th Hour. Chuck Castleberry, Leonardo DiCaprio, Brian Gerber, producers. 2007.
Food, Inc. Robert Kenner, producer. 2008.
Gasland: Can You Light Your Water on Fire? Trish Adlesic, Josh Fox, Molly Gandour, producers. 2010.
If a Tree Falls: A Story of the Earth Liberation Front. Sam Cullman, Marshall Curry, Jo Lapping, producers. 2011.
An Inconvenient Truth. Lawrence Bender and Scott Z. Burns, producers. 2006.
The Island President. Richard Berge and Bonni Cohen, producers. 2011.
Switch: Discover the Future of Energy. Harry Lynch and Scott Tinker, producers. 2012.
Tapped. Michael Walrath, Michelle Walrath, producers. 2009.
Trashed: Candida Brady, Rose Ganguzza, Jeremy Irons, Titus Ogilvy, producers. 2012.

Organizations

350.org: 350.org
EarthFirst!: earthfirst.org
Friends of the Earth: foe.org
Greenpeace: greenpeace.org
NASA: nasa.gov
National Audubon Society: audubon.org
Natural Resources Defense Council: nrdc.org
The Nature Conservancy: nature.org
The Ocean Cleanup: theoceancleanup.org
Our Children's Trust: ourchildrenstrust.org

ALEXANDRA STYRON

The Sea Shepherd Conservation Society:
  seashepherd.org
The Sierra Club: sierraclub.org

IMMIGRATION

Books

*Coyotes: A Journey Through the Secret World
  of America's Illegal Aliens.* Ted Conover.
  Random House, 1988.
*The Death of Josseline: Immigration Stories from
  the Arizona Borderlands.* Margaret Regan.
  Beacon Press, 2010.
A Long Way Gone: Memoirs of a Boy Soldier.
  Ishmael Beah. Sarah Crichton Books, 2008.
*The Lost Boys of Sudan: An American Story
  of the Refugee Experience.* Mark Bixler.
  University of Georgia Press, 2016.
*Toward a Better Life: America's New Immigrants
  in Their Own Words from Ellis Island to the
  Present.* Peter Morton Coan. Prometheus
  Books, 2011.
Vietnamerica: A Family's Journey. GB Tran.
  Villard, 2011.

Documentaries

Documented. Jose Antonio Vargas, Sabrina
  Schmidt Gordon, producers. 2013.
Don't Tell Anyone (No Le Digas a Nadie).
  Mikaela Shwer, Alexandra Nikolchev, Katie
  O'Rourke, producers. 2015.
Homeland: Immigration in America. Jim
  Kirchherr, Anne-Marie Berger, producers. 2012.
Lost Boys of Sudan. Megan Mylan, Jon Shenk,
  producers. 2003.
Rain in a Dry Land. Anne Makepeace, producer.
  2007.
Underwater Dreams. Mary Mazzio, producer. 2014.
Which Way Home. Rebecca Cammisa, producer.
  2009.

Organizations

Define American: defineamerican.com

Families for Freedom: familiesforfreedom.org
Immigrant Defense Project: immdefense.org
International Rescue Committee: rescue.org
PROOF: Media for Social Justice: proof.org
United We Dream: unitedwedream.org

LGBTQIA RIGHTS

Books

*Becoming Visible: A Reader in Gay and Lesbian
  History for High School and College Students.*
  Kevin Jennings. Alyson Books, 1994.
*The Full Spectrum: A New Generation of Writing
  About Gay, Lesbian, Bisexual, Transgender,
  Questioning, and Other Identities.* David
  Levithan, Billy Merrell, editors. Ember, 2006.
Fun Home: A Family Tragicomic. Alison
  Bechdel. Houghton Mifflin, 2006.
*It Gets Better: Coming Out, Overcoming
  Bullying, and Creating a Life Worth Living.*
  Dan Savage, Terry Miller, editors. Dutton,
  2011.
The Perks of Being a Wallflower. Stephen
  Chbosky. Pocket Books, 1999.
*Redefining Realness: My Path to Womanhood,
  Identity, Love & So Much More.* Janet Mock.
  Atria Books, 2014.

Documentaries

Do I Sound Gay? Howard Gertler, David Thorpe,
  producers. 2015.
For the Bible Tells Me So. Daniel G. Karslake,
  producer. 2007.
How to Survive a Plague. Dan Cogan, Howard
  Gertler, producers. 2012.
Stonewall Uprising. Kate Davis, David
  Heilbroner, Mark Samels, producers. 2010.
The Times of Harvey Milk. Richard Schmiechen,
  Rob Epstein, Gregory W. Bex, producers. 1984.

Organizations

ACT UP, AIDS Coalition to Unleash Power:
  actupny.org

American Civil Liberties Union: aclu.org
amfAR (American Foundation for AIDS
    Research): amfar.org
Athlete Ally: athleteally.org
The Audre Lorde Project: alp.org
FIERCE: fiercenyc.org
GLAAD: glaad.org
GLSEN: glsen.org
The Human Rights Campaign: hrc.org
Lambda Legal: lambdalegal.org
Sylvia Rivera Law Project: srlp.org
The Trevor Project: thetrevorproject.org
You Can Play: youcanplayproject.org

RACIAL JUSTICE

Books

American Born Chinese. Gene Luen Yang. First
    Second, 2007.
Between the World and Me. Ta-Nehisi Coates.
    Spiegel & Grau, 2015.
Bury My Heart at Wounded Knee. Dee Brown.
    Holt, Rinehart & Winston, 1970.
The Fire Next Time. James Baldwin. Dial Press,
    1963.
*The Fire This Time: A New Generation Speaks
    about Race*. Jesmyn Ward, editor. Scribner,
    2016.
Just Mercy: A Story of Justice and Redemption.
    Bryan Stevenson. Spiegel & Grau,
    2014.
Narrative of the Life of Frederick Douglass.
    Frederick Douglass. Norton Critical Edition,
    2016.
The New Jim Crow. Michelle Alexander. The
    New Press, 2010.
*Why Are All the Black Kids Sitting Together in
    the Cafeteria?* Beverly Daniel Tatum, PhD.
    Basic Books, 2017.
*The Woman Warrior: Memoirs of a Girlhood
    Among Ghosts*. Maxine Hong Kingston.
    Vintage, 1989.

Articles

"White Privilege: Unpacking the Invisible
    Knapsack." Peggy McIntosh (available at
    nationalseedproject.org). 1989.

Documentaries

The Color of Fear. Lee Mun Wah, producer.
    1994.
Eyes on the Prize. Michael Ambrosino, Alison
    Bassett, John Else, Mark Samels, producers.
    1987.
4 Little Girls. Spike Lee, Samuel Pollard,
    producers. 1997.
The House I Live In. Eugene Jarecki, Sam
    Cullman, Melinda Shopsin, Christopher St.
    John, producers. 2012.
I Am Not Your Negro. Rémi Grellety, Hébert
    Peck, Raoul Peck, producers. 2016.
The Loving Story. Nancy Abraham, Scott
    Berrie, Sheila Nevins, Marshall Sonenshine,
    producers. 2011.
Never Perfect. Regina Park, producer. 2007.
O.J., Made in America. Ezra Edelman, Caroline
    Waterlow, producers. 2016.
13th. Ava DuVernay, Howard Barish, producers.
    2016.

Organizations

American Indian College Fund: collegefund.org
Asian Americans Advancing Justice:
    advancingjustice-la.org
Black Lives Matter Network: blacklivesmatter.
    com
Color of Change: colorofchange.org
National Congress of American Indians: ncai.org
Running Strong for American Indian Youth:
    indianyouth.org
Showing Up for Racial Justice:
    showingupforracialjustice.org
Southerners on New Ground:
    southernersonnewground.org
UnidosUS: UnidosUS.org

RELIGIOUS UNDERSTANDING

Books

Burqas, Baseball, and Apple Pie: Being Muslim in America. Ranya Tabari Idliby. St. Martin's, 2014.

The Complete Maus. Art Spiegelman. Pantheon, 1996.

God's Troublemakers: How Women of Faith Are Changing the World. Katharine Rhodes Henderson. Continuum, 2006.

Interfaith Leadership: A Primer. Eboo Patel. Beacon Press, 2016.

Persepolis. Marjane Satrapi. L'Association, 2000.

Revolution for Dummies: Laughing through the Arab Spring. Bassem Youssef. HarperCollins, 2017.

Documentaries

The Calling. David A. Ranghelli, producer. 2009.

Jesus Camp. Heidi Ewing, Jannat Gargi, Rachel Grady, producers. 2006.

Samsara. Mark Magidson, producer. 2011.

Taqwacore: The Birth of Punk Islam: Daniel Cross, Mila Aung-Thwin, producers. 2009.

Tickling Giants. Sara Taksler, Frederic Rose, Maziar Bahari, Monica Hampton, producers. 2016.

Organizations

Auburn Seminary: auburnseminary.org
CAIR: cair.com
Interfaith Youth Core: ifyc.org
Jewish Voice for Peace: jewishvoiceforpeace.org
Redefy: redefy.org
Religion Communicators Council: religioncommunicators.org
Tanenbaum Center for Interreligious Understanding: tanenbaum.org
Tulsa Changemakers: tulsachangemakers.org

WOMEN'S RIGHTS

Books

The Beauty Myth. Naomi Wolf. Harper Perennial, 2012.

Feminism Is for Everybody: Passionate Politics. bell hooks. Routledge, 2014.

Full Frontal Feminism: A Young Woman's Guide to Why Feminism Matters. Jessica Valenti. Seal Press, 2014.

Here We Are: Feminism for the Real World. Kelly Jensen. Algonquin, 2017.

The Second Sex. Simone de Beauvoir. Vintage edition, 1989.

Shrill. Lindy West. Hachette, 2016.

Sister Outsider: Essays and Speeches. Audre Lorde. Crossing Press, 2007.

We Should All Be Feminists. Chimamanda Ngozi Adichie. Anchor, 2015.

Documentaries

Dark Girls. Bill Duke, D. Channsin Berry, producers. 2011.

Girl Rising. Martha Adams, producer. 2013.

The Hunting Ground. Amy Ziering, producer. 2015.

The Invisible War. Amy Ziering, Tanner King Barklow, producers. 2012.

Miss Representation. Jennifer Siebel Newsom, producer. 2011.

The Punk Singer. Sini Anderson, Tamra Davis, producers. 2013.

She's Beautiful When She's Angry. Mary Dore, Nancy Kennedy, producers. 2014.

Organizations

End Rape on Campus: endrapeoncampus.org
Equality Now: equalitynow.org
Feminist Majority Foundation: feminist.org
National Organization for Women: now.org
Planned Parenthood: plannedparenthood.org
Polaris Project: polarisproject.org

Rape, Abuse & Incest National Network:
    RAINN.org
Shared Hope: sharedhope.org
Sistersong: sistersong.net
Victim Rights Law Center: victimrights.org
Women's Global Empowerment Fund:
    wgefund.org

INTERSECTIONALITY

Books

Ain't I a Woman: Black Women and Feminism.
    bell hooks. Routledge, 2014.
*Colonize This! Young Women of Color on Today's
    Feminism.* Daisy Hernandez. Seal Press,
    2002.

Organizations

Echoing Ida: echoingida.org
Third Wave Fund: thirdwavefund.org

DISABILITY ISSUES

Books

A Disability History of the United States. Kim E.
    Nielsen. Beacon Press, 2013.

*Far from the Tree: Parents, Children, and
    the Search for Identity.* Andrew Solomon.
    Scribner, 2012.

Organizations

The American Association of People with
    Disabilities: aapd.com
Disability Visibility Project: disabilityvisibility
    project.org

HOW TO BE A GOOD ALLY

Organizations

He for She: heforshe.org
Showing Up for Racial Justice (SURJ):
    showingupforracialjustice.org
Straight for Equality: straightforequality.org
White Noise Collective: conspireforchange.org

ACKNOWLEDGMENTS

When I started writing this book, I was super excited, but also a little nervous. There was so much I knew and wanted to say. But there was also a lot I needed to learn. Fast. So, I did a ton of research. And I also asked for a ton of help. *Steal This Country* would not have come together without the contributions of many wonderful people who helped bring the idea to life.

A big heaping thank you, as always, to my agent and friend Esther Newberg who has social justice in her blood and enthusiastically ran with this idea when I brought it to her.

At Viking, many thanks to my editor, Sheila Keenan, who shares my sense of outrage at what is happening out there and who worked so hard to make *Steal This Country* a response to it. Copyeditors Laura Stiers and Janet Pascal saved my butt by both catching errors and making thoughtful suggestions for ways to improve the manuscript. And Kate Renner worked like a demon to bring the whole thing to life with her kickass design.

Speaking of visuals: Jensine Eckwall's charming and excellent spot art perfectly realizes what was little more than a vague idea of mine to enliven the text with images. And Jamie Emmerman totally got what I wanted for photographs, then went a step further, finding amazing pictures and putting them all together with speed and grace.

Closer to home: my *Drumroll-Please-Super-Deluxe* gratitude goes to Lilah Larson. Lilah took time out of a busy touring and recording schedule with her band, Sons of an Illustrious Father, to come on as my assistant and make this book happen fast. Her ideas were invaluable, her contributions incalculable. Lilah's wisdom, humor, and taste are on every page. I literally couldn't have done it without her.

Huge thanks also to my dear friend Annie Silberman Otis who rode to the rescue in my frantic hours, employing her ample skills as a journalist and cheerleader to get the project to the finish line. Peter Schmader was also super helpful, putting in long hours on the research front.

So many people gave their time to draw and write and answer questions for *Steal This Country*. Most of their contributions are here in these pages to see. But some are not, and so they deserve an extra dollop of gratitude for the time spent with me and the wisdom they imparted. Thanks to writer and anti-war activist David Harris for a fascinating interview; to

Judy Gumbo, an original Yippie, who helped hone the art of the political prank and shared some great stories with us; to Andrew Spector, an Interfaith Youth Core alumnus and co-founder of Tulsa Changemakers for the time he took explaining his valuable work; to the women of the San Francisco Young Feminist Alliance for being innovators in youth organizing. And finally, Senator Al Franken: thanks for everything you did for this book and have done for this country.

I am very lucky to have a whole bunch of really smart friends who helped me think through ideas, understand complicated stuff, and get in touch with people I wanted to talk to. It takes a village! In no particular order, I am enormously grateful to: Clara Bingham, Maria Cuomo Cole, Julianne Hoffenberg, Richard Plepler, Ashley Jansen, Michael Lynton, Jamie Alter Lynton, Michael Carlisle, Eric Woolworth, Rick Welts, Peter Sarsgaard, Susanna Aaron, Lee Gelernt, Daniel Kellison, Rory Kennedy, Henry Louis Gates Jr., Abigail Pogrebin, Diane Fitzgerald, Susan Sommer, Ilana Levine, Billy Kimball, Judy Kuhn, Wren Arthur, Linda Semans Donovan, and Susan White.

Thank you to my husband Ed Beason, for inspiring the book's title and inspiring me in all ways. And to my children, Huck and Martha—you make the future look bright.